F@#% the Knot!

How to be a fantastic bridesmaid when you think 'wedding' is a four-letter word.

By Jaqueline Kyle

Published by:

PYP Publishing Group

Address: 725 Fawn Court

City, State Zip: Vacaville, CA 95687

For Further information please visit www.PYPPublishingGroup.com or call: 415-599-4475

F@#% the Knot:

How to be a Fantastic Bridesmaid When You Think "Wedding" is a Four-Letter Word

©Jaqueline Kyle

All rights reserved.

Cover Design and Editor: Jaqueline Kyle

PYP Publishing Group

www.PYPPublishingGroup.com

First Printing: 2012

Table of Contents

Introduction

History

Why on earth does a bride need all of her best friends to help her get down that short little aisle? Why can't she stand by herself to get married? If pressed, I would have guessed that the invention of the bridesmaid was by a not-so-nice bride who wanted to gloat over her matrimonial success by making her single friends stand up in front of the whole procession and pretend to smile while they quietly ate their jealous hearts out. Either that or a way for the father of the bride to pimp out his other daughters to the eligible bachelor's in attendance à la slave market style, "Look at the wares here gents! All available and of breeding age! Never been used!" (Insert cynical laughter here.)

Turns out, neither of my theories were exactly true (but I give myself points for creativity). What I found was much more interesting. The idea of bridesmaids first started in Ancient Rome as a group of similarly dressed women that accompanied the bride to the groom's village and helped defend both the bride's honor and the bride's dowry from the perils of the road. Later, a Roman law changed to require at least 10 witnesses to be in attendance to make a wedding official, thus creating the original "wedding party."

Later down the timeline, some superstitious fool got it into their head that evil spirits attended marriages and those spirits were bent on cursing the marriage! So what is a poor bride to do? Well, why not dress up yourself and all of your friends in the exact same outfit so the evil spirits don't know who to curse! Brilliant! And thus began the tradition of wearing matching dresses. Also, have you ever heard the saying "thrice a bridesmaid, never a bride?" This comes from the belief that the evil spirits slowly poison you as you nobly play "decoy" for three marriages. Yes. Did you know that by agreeing to wear a taffeta dress of questionable taste that you were, in fact, also agreeing to heroically decoy evil spirits and possibly be slowly cursed yourself? Talk about taking one for the team! We bridesmaids are heroes!

F@#% The Knot

It is a good thing that we are heroes because the modern wedding has gone, well, berserk. Weddings are no longer a simple gathering of friends and family, but an insane parade of parties, pastels and layers upon layers of tulle. The average wedding costs upwards of $25,000 – about five times more than I spent on my first car. The quest to tie the knot has become a multi-billion dollar a year industry full of brides trying to make their day unique, special, memorable and driving themselves and their loved ones to drink in the process.

Between Pinterest, Bridezillas, Say Yes to the Dress, and more magazines and websites dedicated to wedding preparation than you can shake a stick at, the temptation to go overboard has reached epic proportions for brides everywhere. What's worse is that the brides have begun to expect the same excess from their entourage, demanding multiple showers, destination bachelorette parties and more. Is it any wonder that 'wedding' has become a four-letter word for the bridesmaids?

What is a bridesmaid?

So what is a modern day bridesmaid? We wear many, many hats... and dresses of a questionable nature. The modern day bridesmaid is the thrower of parties, the calmer of nerves, the tactful negotiator of fashion, the leader of the conga line and the small voice that asks if maybe the wedding planner has gone a little overboard. We are the last minute troubleshooters, the women who get things done; we are the ones that can be called on in the clinch.

This book is for the first-time bridesmaid or maid of honor who isn't quite sure what being a bridesmaid entails. It is full of practical advice from someone who has led the conga line a time or two herself. It's also full of wit and what not to do, because weddings are fraught with etiquette and situations to make fun of. And if you're going to be a bridesmaid, you might as well have fun, right?

The biggest advice I can give you is to read this book now. Learn what you have committed yourself to and (more importantly) how to balance practical bridesmaids duties with the excess of the modern bridal industry. The more time you have to prepare, the easier this will be for you, the other bridesmaids and, of course, your bride.

Good luck fellow bridesmaid. You are embarking on a journey that will be full of humor, frustration and memories for a lifetime. Embrace the chaos!

Jaqueline Kyle
Maid of Honor, Extraordinaire

Chapter 1
Will you be my... bridesmaid?

Before you Accept

Your friend and/or sister has just called. (Yes, "sister" and "friend" are not always the same thing.) She's bubbling with excitement because GUESS WHAT? She is finally getting married! And won't you please, please, puh-lease be her bridesmaid?

You're reading this book, so I'm going to guess that your answer was "yes," right? Well this is my moment to play the devil's advocate. Yep, I'm going to try to talk you out of participating in this blessed event. Not because I'm a mean wedding wrecker, but to fully inform you as to what you've signed up for.

Time

There is only a finite amount of time in your day, week and month. You have your own responsibilities. Do you love or at least like this bride enough to make time to:

♥ Attend engagement parties, bridal showers, bachelorette parties and any other cake-tasting, venue-touring event that she might ask you to appear at.

♥ Go dress shopping for both the bride's dress as well as the bridesmaid dresses.

♥ Listen on the phone as the bride endlessly discusses flower selections, seating charts and the musical playlists.

♥ Run errands, especially at the last minute.

Your time is expected if you say "yes" to joining the ranks of her bridesmaids. It's not negotiable. If you have a busy career, family, husband, kids of your own, you need to consider your time. Are you going to be there for your bride or are you going to cause her more trouble in the long run? Be honest with yourself.

Money

The next consideration is financial. Weddings are expensive. Do you like the bride enough to spend money on:

♥ A dress you probably won't like and will never wear again.

♥ Ditto: shoes, accessories, etc.

♥ If you live far away, plane tickets to attend the major events.

♥ Your share of the bridal shower and bachelorette party.

At the very least, there needs to be a discussion with the bride about costs. What does she expect the dress will cost? Does she want her bridal shower at a friend's house or does she expect high tea at the snooty café downtown? Does she expect the bachelorette party to be a tour of the local dive bars or a three-day cruise to Mexico? Every bride is different. Some want MULTIPLE bridal showers because they know so many people. Make sure that you have a good idea of what you are committing your wallet to.

Staying in the Game

Let's face it, your friend and/or sister is going to cease being either one for the foreseeable future. You're going to lose her into a bridal black hole. If you are game for long conversations about spanx and the difference between periwinkle and lavender then you will still be in rotation on her phone list. But do not expect her to ask how you are doing, what's new in your life or partake in whatever it is that you normally talk about. She's gone down the bridal black hole, and she is not going to be coming back anytime soon.

When Everyone You Know is Getting Married.

It happens. Engagement can get in the water and suddenly everyone you know is heading down the aisle. And you are so darn popular that you've been asked to participate in all of them.

This actually happened to a friend of mine who found herself in EIGHT weddings in one year. She actually had to take on a second job to manage the financial burden.

Money is a real financial consideration when deciding to participate in a wedding. If you are asked to participate in multiple weddings, you should really make a decision about which ones are most important to you. The financial obligations can be burdensome for one, never mind eight!

You need to decide, how much do you want to participate in a relationship with this friend and/or sister who has been suddenly and terribly afflicted with bride-itis? (By the way, it truly is a sickness. It lasts the entire engagement and finally let's up somewhere around the first anniversary. If she gets pregnant, the whole thing starts again until sometime after the baby's first birthday.) If you decide to stick with your current friendship, you are going to need a boatload of patience. If you decide to bail, it can kill your friendship. And if you only do a halfway job, it can also be detrimental to your relationship. If this is only a so-so friendship, it might make more sense to walk away now.

Politics

Finally, you need to consider your politics. If you are family with the bride there will be consequences if you A.) decline to participate or B.) do a poor job in your duties as a bridesmaid. Rock, I'd like to introduce you to Hard Place. By declining to be a bridesmaid, your sister or cousin or whomever, may carry a grudge that you will hear about at every Christmas and family reunion from now until the end of time. There is no escaping it. Just accept her invitation graciously and live up to your duties (and if you can manage it, do it cheerfully).

Should you decline

If you decide to turn your bride down, you need to do it with tact. Explain your reason and (if willing) that you would like to fill a less demanding role, like being in charge of the guestbook. A decline needs to be done before the planning goes too far and with as much honesty as you can muster. Send a gift with your decline, it smooth's the way.

Bridesmaid vs. Maid (or Matron) of Honor

For those of you that are in the business world, marriage is like a merger. Single Lady Co is merging with Single Stud LLC to form Happy Couple, Inc. The merger is stressful and the CEO of Single Lady Co is hiring a Maid of Honor to be the VP of Bridesmaid Relations until the merger is completed. The VP of Bridesmaid Relations has many projects to complete and must get the bridesmaids in her department to help her complete them. Projects to be completed include, but are not limited to: choosing a dress that everyone can wear and ordering them, organizing and throwing bridal shower(s) and a bachelorette party.

Simply speaking, a Maid of Honor's responsibility is to lead. She is supposed to get every bridesmaid's phone number and start dialing. She needs to get everyone on the same page, get a consensus, and start delegating responsibility.

When to RUN!

Participating in a wedding should not come with a contract. We've heard of brides that kick a pregnant bridesmaid to the curb because she wouldn't look as "aesthetically pleasing" in the photos. We've heard of brides requiring her attendants to sign a contract that they will not get a tan, cut their hair, or gain weight before the big day. We've heard of brides requiring bridesmaids to lose 5 -20 lbs. These are all reasons that I would tell a bride where to stick it, but there is a new trend sweeping the nation... Botox, breast enhancements and chemical peels.

Seriously. There are brides that are asking their closest friend to change their physical appearances PERMANENTLY for a wedding that they aren't even getting married at. I'm not exactly sure how this conversation goes, because a contract that you won't cut your hair says, "I love you exactly the way you are" but a request to plump your lips, smooth out your crows feet and push up your bra sizes says, "I love you but you aren't perfect and I want you to change for me."

Okay, you are going to be standing up next to her in a dress that probably won't be flattering and there are going to be lots of people looking at you. Fine. You want to do what you can to look good. That's your decision. If you want to go through treatments and skin regiments, it should be 100% something you decide to do for yourself and only yourself. The bride has NO SAY.

If your bride asks you to get a boob job for the big day so you will look better in the dress and in the photos, you have my permission to use any words that come to your head, whether tactful or hurtful. Perhaps the bride might consider choosing a different dress, PhotoShopping the pictures or just taking a giant helping of "get the hell over yourself?" Yes, she may be paying $25,000+ for "her day" but it's just one day. She's asking you to make changes that will effect your for months, if not the rest of your life. Enough said.

If you are a bridesmaid, your job is to suggest ideas and offer help to the maid of honor. It doesn't matter if you have known the bride longer, have a better idea of what the bride would want, or just don't like the maid of honor. Since you both have agreed to participate in this torture, I'm sure you'll find some common ground to work on.

When in Doubt
- ♥ Send the bride a congratulations note.
- ♥ Discuss budget and expectations with the bride.
- ♥ Collect all of the bridesmaid's contact details.

Odd Facts
At their 1955 wedding, Liz Taylor and Mike Todd were accompanied down the aisle by best man Eddie Fisher and the matron of honor was his wife, Debbie Reynolds. In 1959, Eddie left Debbie for Liz and became husband number four!

Chapter 2
Your Duties

Frankly, this whole book is about your duties as a bridesmaid or maid of honor. So don't get super excited that this is a short chapter. This chapter is just a brief overview of the things you didn't know you were agreeing to do when you said, "Yes."

Buyer of Dress

The first time I was a bridesmaid I was shocked. Not only did I have to wear a dress I didn't want, I also had to purchase it! What? That's right. As a participant in the blessed event, you are going to have to submit to purchasing a dress of questionable taste and wear it with gusto. And to add insult to injury, at some point during the primping, wedding or reception, you are going to look over at one of the other bridesmaids and realize: she looks much better in that dress than you do. At that moment, your only option will be to drink yourself into a stupor. With any luck, temporary amnesia will set in.

This exact thing happened to me, come to think of it. I was a college student with a freshman 15 that was holding on stubbornly in my junior year, and she was an amateur body builder. Guess who looked better in their bridesmaid dress? I drank all of the champagne on the table, missed the chair that was pulled out for me and ended up crashing to the floor, in a (thankfully) discreet corner. I claimed that the champagne had a bad reaction with my system and my parents (who were in attendance) still ask over a decade later if "I'm sure" before they will offer me a flute at family occasions. On the flipside of this, as I was primping for a different wedding, I noticed that another bridesmaid's bodice was way too tight and she was rather boob-a-ricffic. At that moment I decided that no one was going to notice me at all, and proceeded to have a great time.

Hers vs. Yours - A Diagram of Dresses

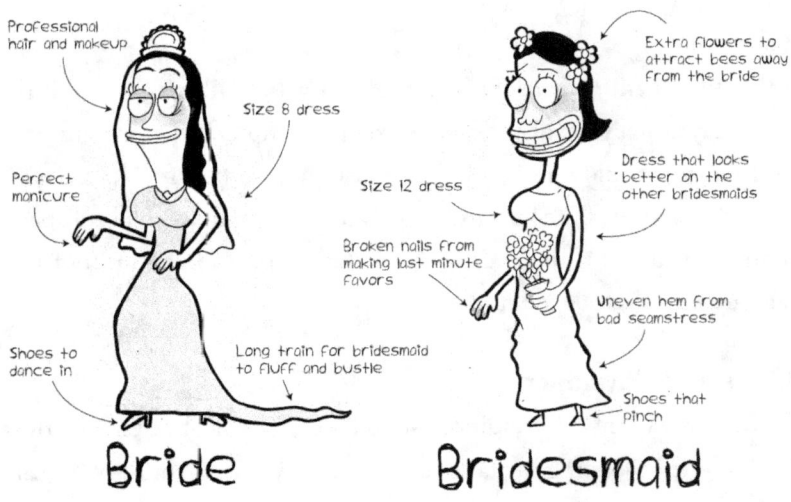

Thrower of Parties

This is my favorite part of being a bridesmaid. I will gladly take on the dangers of bridesmaid duty for the opportunity to get a bunch of people together and make them compliment my cheese spread. Totally balances the scale in my book, because my cheese spread is usually terrible but the guests are required to be polite.

You will be expected to participate, if not plan at least two parties, and you will likely end up attending at least five. The events you will be responsible for (with your fellow bridesmaids) are the bridal shower and bachelorette party (the other three are the engagement party, rehearsal dinner and wedding reception).

In case you didn't know, bridal showers are classy. They usually take place during the daylight; you invite the bride's mother and Great Aunt Ida. There is no vulgar talk and the stories you tell do not involve ex-boyfriends and the night you and the bride closed that bar in New Orleans. There are a lot of pastels at the bridal shower and you can talk publicly about what went on during the party. You can post pictures of the festivities on Facebook. You can even tag the participants.

On the other hand, bachelorette parties can get as wild as you want them to be. They usually involve heavy makeup, trampy clothes and under no circumstances should Great Aunt Ida ever hear a word of it. Alcohol is your friend and it is one of the few times you can walk around with plastic penises in public. Pictures, if there are any, end up in private albums and by no means are they ever tagged on Facebook.

Addresser of Envelopes
I'm not sure when this tradition started. Of all the bridesmaid duties, helping address wedding invitations has to be my least favorite. Why can't a bride write out all two or three hundred envelopes herself? Well, because she doesn't have to, obviously.

Fortunately for me, my handwriting is atrocious. Literally, I can't even read my own penmanship. It made my third grade teacher wail in disgust. So when it comes time to address envelopes, I usually end up doing two or three, until the bride finally agrees that my handwriting is indeed, the ugliest thing she has ever seen. From there I usually volunteer to refill people's glasses, tell jokes, and give hand massages when someone's hand cramps up.

Regardless of whether you are a calligraphy queen or a cursive flunkout like me, you will be asked to help fill out wedding invitations. Both the outer and the inner envelopes are going to have to be filled out and with an average wedding having upwards of 150 guests, that's a lot of writing. Get ready to do your part.

Runner of Errands

Errand running can be overwhelming or a much needed reprieve depending on your bride. Some brides are delegators and have a list of things for each bridesmaid to do. Others are control freaks and the day before (or day of) the wedding they are looking at a list of things they cannot possibly accomplish on their own and are tearfully freaking out.

I was maid of honor to one such bride, who wanted every detail of the wedding to be a surprise and ended up with a huge list of things to do that she trusted to no one because it would "ruin the surprise." Well, there were tears and finally a wrestling match to get her to release her death grip on the to-do list, which was divvied up among the bridesmaids and accomplished in very short order.

To successfully fill your role as a runner of errands, you need to communicate with your bride. Offer your help early. Let the bride know what your availability is and when you would be willing to do a few things on her behalf. If she asks too much, set boundaries. Explain what is already on your plate and what deadlines you are working with. The cardinal rule here is to not flake. If you agree to do something, you have to do it or you have to delegate it to someone else. Under no circumstances should you add to the stress of the bride – because a bitchy bride makes everyone's lives miserable.

Social Maven

Some people are meant to entertain the room. They float from conversation to conversation, delighting people with their wit as they go. Some people (ahem: raises hand) are shy by nature and would rather people watch from a corner of the room. If you are a natural corner dweller, you need to prepare yourself: you will not have that option at the wedding reception. You will be wearing a dress that says, "Come talk to me, I know what's going on." People will come to you with questions, they will want to talk to you because the bride isn't available, they will want to chat because they are just so darn happy (and drunk). If you are someone who feels perpetually lost for words, check out the news, the weather and destination of the honeymoon. These are usually safe topics that can sustain you through a conversation!

When in Doubt

- ♥ Order your dress three or more months before the wedding.
- ♥ Schedule at least two fittings.
- ♥ Ask the bride what you can do to help.
- ♥ Prepare to make small talk with guests at various events.

Odd Facts

Listerine popularized the saying "Always a bridesmaid, never a bride" in an ad campaign that featured a 30-something woman with bad breath.

Chapter 3
Here comes the Dress!

So the bride has asked you to stand next to her on the big day and you find that you have said yes, perhaps against your better judgment. What's next? Well the dress, of course! This chapter is full of tips on how to find the best dress for you and the bride, without sticking your foot in your mouth!

Dress Shopping

There may not be a date set yet, but by god, your bride is going to find that dress now. That way she knows exactly how much weight she will need to lose! Seriously, I don't know why the dress is the number one priority, but I guarantee that your bride will start looking before she's had time to flash that newly sized ring to her closest friends and relations. And ultimately, someone will say, "Well as long as you have a dress, you just need to find a minister and you are all set!" As if.

But unrealistic and annoying sayings aside, here's the lowdown on the dress shopping. In theory, it's fun. In reality, it's a purgatory that you will want to escape as quickly as possible. There are giant stores that specialize only in mass produced wedding dresses and they keep those wedding dresses in plastic sheets lined up like soldiers in row after row of taffeta, lace and silk. These dresses are so constructed and pushed so close together, that in they can stand on their own and the hangers are there merely to keep them aligned. There are millions upon millions of styles, colors and fashions. Yes, I said colors! Brides are choosing beige or white with ribbons or whatever strikes their fancy these days. Because choosing if your dress needs a train, sleeveless, strapless, lace, A-line, princess cut, empire waist, etc. was too easy. Now they want brides to choose colors too.

When You Eat Your Words

In the 70's, my father married my mother in a powder blue tuxedo that he still insists was the bee's knees. Looking at the pictures of the day, after I finally stopped howling in laughter at his pastel tuxedo, I turned my attention to my mother and her attendants. Mom was glowing. She looked absolutely radiant on the day. But her bridesmaids were attired in what my mother described as "colors of the spring." Each bridesmaid was decked out in a different head-to-toe pastel color. They looked like giant Easter eggs. I laughed and teased again until I was wiping my eyes with tears.

Fast forward to a dressing room in a bridal warehouse some years in the future. My sister is the bride and has her dress in-hand. My mother and I are perusing the bridesmaid dresses. I point out the new fashion of choosing a color and letting the bridesmaids choose the dress style that best suits their body. Apparently that was too close to "colors of the spring" and I found myself pummeled by my mother with indignant comments about what's fashionable now won't be later and her grandchildren will make fun of my sister for the rest of her life, blah, blah, blah. My sister wanders over to find out why my mother's voice has raised an octave, and quickly assures her that under no circumstances would she trust her bridesmaids to picking their own styles. And that is how I ended up in a periwinkle floor-length monstrosity on her wedding day. Lesson to take away: never incense the mother of the bride. She can be your greatest ally or your worst enemy!

Ah, but I digress. The bridal store will smell of plastic sheeting and will inevitably be playing some acoustic, overly peppy version of a song that you used to like, but now it has been so tainted by flutes and piano overtures that your ears will melt if you ever listen to it again. It is a white (and beige) purgatory. To spend as little of your life as possible in these warehouses of horror, try to discuss what the bride is looking for before you get there. To help, buy a bridal magazine or three for the bride and let her get an idea of what she wants on her own time. Call it an engagement gift, but really, this gift is for you. You are giving yourself the gift of time not spent in a plastic smelling white warehouse with bad music.

When you do get to the bridal warehouse of horrors, expect to be greeted by a "consultant." The dress consultant will be the bride's guide as she inspects the dress soldiers lined up and down the warehouse. She will ask the bride for her input and completely ignore you and the other bridesmaids, but will probably be very friendly to the mother-of-the-bride, as she is most likely going to be the one paying. These women work on commission, so they are going to try every trick in the book to make that bride commit to a dress. Therefore, this dress consultant is your new best friend.

You probably won't have much to do but wander at first. The dress consultant will start pulling dresses and sticking them in a dressing room. This is where your work begins. Scope out the dressing area and throw your purse, jacket, etc. on the second best seat you can find. The mother of the bride will take the absolute best seat, and you'll look like a heel if you try to knock the old lady out of her perch. But claim your seat early, especially if there is a bunch of you. There's usually only two good chairs, and the rest of the bridesmaids will be stuck with benches with no backs, or have to stand and lean against the display cases.

So the bride is in the changing room, getting acquainted with the helpfully supplied strapless bra (it's available for purchase! Remember: the consultant works on commission). This is your moment to strike up the bridesmaid dress conversation. Has anyone thought about how it should look? Don't bother trying to come to a consensus on color. The bride is inevitably going to choose that to go with whatever color with wedding will be. This is your moment to size up which girls will be in your alliance. Who wants full-length, and who looks better in tea-length? What is the feeling on strapless vs. some sort of support? The bride might have ideas for her attendants, but if everyone is a different body type, she is going to have to take input from someone. Best it be you and the attendants who agree with you. If someone says they don't care what it looks like, they are lying and may not know it yet. Count them in the bride's corner and keep on with your Machiavellian ways.

When Complaining Goes Too Far

Lavender, periwinkle, whatever the color that dress was, I hated it. I made it known to one and all that whichever shade of purple they wanted to call that taffeta nightmare, I was only wearing it because I loved my sister, the bride. I found ways to work it into the conversation. When people asked about the bridesmaid dresses, I would see my sister stiffen out of the corner of my eye. As the wedding got closer, she would hold her breath too.

I eventually caught onto the fact that I had pushed it too far. Unfortunately, I didn't catch on until I wore a purple top six months after the wedding and my sister accusingly shouted, "You DO wear purple!" Ouch. As far as I know, she never actually cried about my abhorrence of her dress choice, however, should I ever decide that pastel purple is my color; I will never hear the end of it. If you want to keep all color choices available to your entire future wardrobe, learn from my mistake and be a bit more tactful when asked about the bridesmaid dress.

When the bride comes out in her first few tries, wait to see what she says first. If she hated it, she would be trying a different one on in the dressing room right then. So saying something like "That's atrocious," is not going to go over well. Even if you do think it's atrocious, it might be better to say, "I don't know about that one. What else do you have to try on?" Most people save the one they are most looking forward to for last. When it is the right dress, she's going to kind of glow. It's weird, but true, I have no explanation for it. You're job is not to dress her up how you would like to be looking on your wedding day. Your job is only to steer her away from a dress that is unflattering, encourage her if she feels discouraged and agree with her when she has already made up her mind.

Tactful Tips for Her Dress

The bride wants to feel beautiful and comfortable in her dress. On the way to finding that dress you need to be tactful. You don't want to be the one that made the bride cry in the dressing room!

Don't Say It!

The bride invited a friend from out of town to her final dress fitting. The bride came out of the dressing room in full regalia and her friend... failed.

"It's just not my style."

The bride was crushed. Her friend didn't like her dress. With those five little words, her friend made her doubt her own taste and destroyed her confidence. She went back to the dressing room and cried as she took off her beloved dress.

Her friend then followed her back into the dressing room to comfort her by saying that it probably wasn't too late to "fix" the dress. (The bride, by the way, looked amazing in her dress.) Rather than fix the dress, the bride ditched the friend.

If you want to stay friends with the bride, remember that your job is to be supportive, regardless of whether her choice is "your style."

If in doubt, ask her what she thinks first. You can't go wrong there. Questions, in general, are usually pretty safe. "What do you think of that broach in the back?" might be a way to draw her attention to a god-awful train. "I don't know, could you go down a size?" is a polite way to say your boobies are hanging out. If the color makes her look all wrong, ask her if she sees herself getting a tan before the wedding. If she looks strapped in so tight she can hardly breathe, ask her to sit down. When in doubt, always preface your statements with "I don't know" or "I'm not sure" and then say whatever it is that you don't like in the nicest way you can think of.

Bridesmaid Dress Shopping

There are at least two other bridesmaids and probably more. You most likely have different skin tones and body types. The bride has her dress and has turned her attention to her attendants. This is your moment to jump in!

Volunteer. Be the proverbial dummy and volunteer to model the dresses for the bride and (if present) the other bridesmaids. If the other bridesmaids are there, they will probably jump in at this point and try to share your dressing room, but you've already established yourself first.

Many of these bridal stores have a small section dedicated to bridesmaid dresses. Find out what color the bride is considering and try that on first, regardless of style. If the color makes you look washed out or green, this is your first, best chance to get her to change her mind. These big bridal stores are going to try to convince you to go for style, that you can order the dress in whatever color the bride decides on. Big Mistake. Make the bride see what that color is going to look like on you FIRST. The style is going to be a debate that is not going to be settled the first day. The color could be – make sure it goes in your favor!

Try on whatever dresses the bride requests of you. If it is god-awful, all the better. A picture is worth a thousand words, right? Well by trying on a few unflattering dresses, you gain brownie points for being a good sport, and once the bride sees that her taste just doesn't suit you, she will be more willing to hear your suggestions. Play along to get along until you can sneak a dress of your choosing into the dressing room.

Once a consensus is reached on the bridesmaid dresses, you are going to have a deadline for going in and ordering your dress. Usually it is ordered three months or more before the wedding day. This will get your dress to the store and available for alterations before the big day. Order your dress on time – for the sanity of the bride, and therefore yourself.

What Size Are You Again?

Here's a little known fact about bridal wear. The bridal dresses run large and the bridesmaid dresses run small. So what does that mean? Well if you and your bestie, the bride, are both a size 10 in the real world, when it comes to dress shopping, she will magically be a size 8 (yay! I MUST buy this dress! I'm an 8!) and you will magically be a size 12 (I can't believe I have to spend money on this!).

It's all part of a vast conspiracy by brides every where to wage psychological warfare on their attendants so that they are the only woman at that altar that feels good about themselves. Cut the tag out as soon as possible.

Tactful Tips for Your Dress

The trick with your dress is to ask for the bride's help. She's in charge anyway, but you'll avoid butting heads if you are coming to her with your concerns rather than laying down a laundry list of styles you are unwilling to even try on.

Point out the flaws that you are going to need her consideration covering. If you have a bad scar, make sure she knows it. If you are a redhead, point out what colors are never going to work. You are the expert on dressing you. You know how to make yourself look good. Enlist the bride's help in at least covering the things that you can't bear to show in public.

When in Doubt

- ♥ Go with the bride to shop for her dress
- ♥ Don't bother trying to get her to even acknowledge that you need a dress until she either A.) has a dress or B.) has tried on every wedding dress in a 100-mile radius.
- ♥ Offer constructive comments about the dress, style etc.
- ♥ Try to find a happy medium for all of the bridesmaids

Odd Facts

Princess Diana's wedding dress had a 25-foot train and 10,000 pearls sewn into it. It took five months of dress fittings to learn how to walk in it!

Chapter 4
Party Time!

Weddings are not a one-day event. They are a series of parties that begin at engagement and go on past the wedding reception to brunch and (much later) anniversary parties. This chapter is your guide to the pre-wedding festivities – some of which, you will probably be in charge of!

Engagement Party - A Wedding Reception Without the Wedding.
Engagement parties are optional and are usually thrown if the engagement is expected to exceed a year. The engagement party is scheduled for one to three months after the engagement and I think was invented by disapproving mother-in-laws trying to give their sons a preview of the bridezilla to come. My other theory is that it is for milking more gifts out of the blessed event – but that could just be me being cynical.

The engagement party could be very formal, or (if you're lucky) it could be as simple as a backyard barbeque. You'll probably be able to tell by the invitations (that you helped address) but if in doubt, ask the bride. Your role at this party is going to be more involved in setup than anything else. You will probably be arranging tables and wrestling with the chocolate fountain in the hours before the guests arrive.

Engagement parties are a dry run for the big day, so size up your bride now. Is she handling the stress well? Is she communicating what she needs help with? Is she happy? Or is she crying in the corner and mumbling about eggshell tablecloths instead of ivory? Take mental notes and use them to prepare yourself (and her) for the big day. If she takes too much on herself and doesn't tell people what she needs help with, the bridesmaids are going to need to come up with a strategy to avoid a repeat on the wedding day.

Things They Never Tell You...

1. Throwing parties is expensive. Invitations, food, drink, decorations, favors... it all adds up mind-bogglingly fast. Which leads us to...

2. No one ever chips in. Not what they owe anyway. Bridesmaids show up with a couple bucks to toss in like it's a college keg party. And just like college, what they kick in doesn't cover what they drink. And you have no recourse because...

3. They are her friends, not yours. A good time with your friends might include kegstands and beer bongs, but a good time with her friends might be sipping wine and smelling cheese (or vice versa). When in Rome you are going to have to suck it up because...

4. These are the same friends you are going to see at EVERY occasion from bridal showers to baby showers to (if they stick around that long) graduations. It's going to be a very awkward twenty some-odd years if you alienate her friends now, even if they deserve it. Which leads us to the most important point....

5. Don't set the bar too high. You're going to be throwing parties for the bride with the exact same guest list almost annually for the foreseeable future. Don't break the bank on the first one!

The guest list at an engagement party is usually a preview of the wedding, with immediate family, attendants and close friends. They are there to help celebrate and congratulate the happy couple. Unless otherwise specified by the bride, once the party starts, you just need to mingle and chat with the guests. Enjoy - this will most likely be the party with the least amount of responsibility for you and your fellow bridesmaids!

Bridal Shower

The bridal shower is a time-honored tradition and while the sarcastic part of me wants to say that it is purely thrown in pursuit of more presents, I know that this is not the ONLY reason. Actually, if you think about it, the wedding is a hectic-crazy-fantastic-overwhelming day for the couple. And with 100+ guests and a three-hour reception, the most time any guest can expect to share with the happy couple is about 30 seconds.

A bridal shower is an opportunity for a more intimate gathering of well-wishers. The guests tend to be close friends and family of the bride. These people do genuinely care for the bride, enough that they are willing to come and spend more money on presents for her. And if the party happens to drive the bridesmaids closer to the poorhouse, well, what can I say.

Timing

Bridal showers are usually two to three months before the big day. Why so far in advance? Well, the closer it gets to the big day, the more the bride is going to be overwhelmed and freaking out. So she probably won't enjoy a Saturday afternoon being monopolized right before the wedding when she could be running errands. Also, the typical questions from guests are things like, "How is the planning going? What are your colors? What does your dress look like?" If she doesn't know the answers, she's going to leave the party freaking out. So an extra two months to sort those details out would be a good thing.

Venue

Where is your party going to be held? A bridal shower usually takes place in someone's home. A friend or mother-of-the-bride's home will do, but you want to stay out of the bride's home as much as possible (there are usually color swatches and bridal magazines on every available surface, she will flip out at the added stress of cleaning). If you know of someone who is naturally neat and tidy and doesn't mind opening their home, it's perfect.

The other way to go is a restaurant or teashop. Ideally you want some place classy that has a private room and won't try to rush you out. If you choose a public venue keep in mind two things. One, any games, memories or roasts are going to have to be PG-13 or less. Two, you are still hosting so you and your bridesmaids will be expected to pick up the tab.

Expectations

So as the hostess of this party, what is expected of you? Well you are the supplier of food, drink and fun!

Food

Whether you are going to provide snacks or a full-on meal is going to be dependent on the time you chose for the party. If the bridal shower is scheduled to start at noon, guests will expect lunch. If it is scheduled for 3, guests will expect snacks. Snacks are cheaper and there are usually leftovers for later.

Be sure to consult with the bride and bridesmaids. The menu should be food that the bride enjoys. In addition, there are a plethora of food allergies that guests may be concerned about. Gluten, shellfish, peanuts, strawberries, are all triggers for certain people. It doesn't mean that shrimp platters are off the menu, just that you should have a variety of food available. Also, when handling food, make sure not to cross-contaminate allergens (i.e. cut shrimp with the same knife used for the deli slices, or having only one serving spoon for multiple dishes).

Drinks

It's a good idea to have a variety of drinks for the guests to choose from. Think lemonade, sparkling water, iced tea, etc. However, dependent on the age of the guests and/or religious beliefs, you may or may not want to have soda and/or alcohol. If you aren't sure, consult with the bride. Also, toasts are traditional and a great touch. If for some reason a bottle of champagne is not appropriate, apple cider will do (don't forget the champagne flutes!).

Note: This is not the bachelorette party. No one is supposed to get drunk. Save the Jell-O shots and kegstands for a different day, ladies.

Share the program

I hope you are not throwing this party alone. Make sure everyone involved in hosting knows the program. Most showers last two to three hours. The whole thing doesn't need to be planned out to the minute, just know what order things are going to go in. For example:

- ↻ 12-12:30: Guests arrive and visit.
- ↻ 12:30-1:00: Eat
- ↻ 1:00-1:15: Game 1
- ↻ 1:15-1:30: Game 2
- ↻ 1:30- 2:00: Open Gifts
- ↻ 2:00- ?: Desserts, Pictures, and Guests Leave.

You won't need to keep to the exact schedule, often times the next event will start when there is a lull in the conversation. Keep an eye on your guests and if they are running out of things to talk about or looking bored, start the next phase of your program.

Invitations

Invitations should go out at least a month in advance of the party. Guests need to be able to plan for it and have time to get the perfect gift. Get the guest list and addresses from the bride in plenty of time to send out the invitations. If time is running short and the bridal shower guests are only her closets friends from high school and college, you can probably get away with sending an E-vite.

On the invitation itself, you need to have the basics: where, when, in honor of (the bride) and who to RSVP to. Often times guests will RSVP directly to the bride, so touch base with her frequently to keep a good head count. If the bride has already registered, it is a good idea to include where in the invitation. Either write it on the invitation itself or print a small separate note with the details (which could save you a lot of time) to stuff inside the envelope along with the invitation.

Finally, if the party has some sort of theme (see Themes), it's best to have invitations that reflect that theme. If a game is going to require some preparation by the guests (see Games), it is also prudent to include anything required in the invitation.

Note: Anyone invited to the shower should also be invited to the wedding. If the bride has given you a list of 25+ names, remind her of that.

Themes

Somehow it's not enough to just throw a party. I'm not sure why, but some brides want a theme. Now if you weren't paying attention in English class, a theme is an idea that is used throughout the course of a book, or in this case, a bridal shower. For example, if you wanted to use teddy bears as a theme, the invitations would have teddy bears on them, the decorations at the party would include stuffed bears and the desserts might be bear-shaped cookies.

What teddy bears have to do with getting married, I'm not sure, but sometimes a bride has always been obsessed with something random, like teddy bears, and her friends just go with it. This can also make for a very personalized and fun party. For example, I've been told that I will soon be invited to a pirate-themed shower and will be required to speak like a pirate for the duration of the party. It's offbeat and wacky and something I can certainly get behind, because parties should be fun!

My big warning on themes is that they can be expensive. Someone gets an idea and suddenly you have to have plates that match the invitations that match the wall decorations and on and on and on. There's a whole industry of pre-packaged themes out there, some pricier that others. You don't need to buy the paper plates that have the exact same style of balloons that are on the invitation. If it's going to save you a sum of money, go with the solid colored plates at the party store. The only criticism you'll get is if you totally buy the Halloween plates from the clearance rack and try to pass them off as part of your teddy bear theme.

Here a few themes I've done or seen pulled off well.

High Tea

The high tea party can be done at a destination location like a teashop or hotel and can also be done at home for less. In general it involves a variety of sweets and finger sandwiches as well as tea. I've done this theme at a personal residence, borrowing mismatched teacups and saucers from family, friends and neighbors. I borrowed three-tiered tea trays and made up scones and sandwiches and a friend made some chocolate dipped strawberries. Another friend had inherited her grandmother's hat collection and as each guest arrived, she was to pick out her old-fashioned hat to drink tea in. The pictures turned out fantastic! Party games revolved mostly around being a "lady" and each guest received a teapot shaped spoon holder for her favor.

Disney

If your bride is into the magic of Disney, this theme should be fairly easy to execute. Disney is the master of marketing and has Princess themed party products for any occasion. Most brides who love Disney have collectables that can be used to decorate the party. One of the brides I threw a party for was obsessed with Cinderella and had several snow globes and figurines that made excellent table decorations. Disney trivia is a typical game at these parties and usually someone unexpected dominates! Word of Warning: Disney products can be a bit pricier than most out there.

Kitchen Parties

I have seen the kitchen party theme done two different ways. The more traditional route is to send the invitation with a blank recipe card and a request for the guest to fill it out with their favorite recipe and bring it to the party. The guests will usually cherry pick the kitchen items from the gift registry and bring bouquets of spatulas and ladles as well as boxes of pots and pans and that mandolin slicer the bride registered for but will never use.

The less traditional route is to throw a Princess House or Pamper Chef (or Celebrate Home, etc., etc., etc.) party. At these parties the guests don't bring gifts but buy the gifts at the party, as well as whatever they want to purchase for themselves. You would only consider throwing one of these if your bride really wanted to furnish her entire kitchen from one source. Typically a registry of what the bride really wants circulates the party. Guests can go in together to purchase larger items for the bride or make individual purchases. The major problem I have seen at these types of parties is that the "Tupperware" sales person wants to do their typical sales presentation and have the undivided attention of the audience. It defeats the purpose of spending one-on-one time with the bride if you can't speak with her or any other guests. If you go this route, talk to the presenter about a limited demonstration or no demonstration. Set the expectations before the day so everyone knows the game plan!

Games/Entertainment

Every party needs games! I'm actually not kidding or being sarcastic on this at all. There will likely be a huge age difference at the party, from young girls the bride used to babysit to Great Aunt Ida who will recall changing the bride's diapers. There are going to be people there who only know the bride and no one else. Rather than just have a room of women all staring at each other, games are a great way to get people interacting and gives them a subject (other than the bride) to talk about. For my parties, I usually go with one game that will run through the length of the party (i.e. "Lady" games below) and then two interactive activities that have a shorter duration (i.e. TP dress or trivia). In addition to my suggestions, there are also a plethora of game and bridal shower activities online.

"Lady" Games

Opposite to what you might guess, lady games revolve around NOT being a lady and calling other women on their lady-like behavior. The most popular of these is "the leg cross." Each guest receives three clothing pins (or any number you want, really) to attach to her clothes. If a guest crosses her legs during the party, another guest can claim a pin from her and add it to her own collection. By the end of the party, usually one guest has taken this game and run with it - resulting in a clear winner of the game.

Other versions of this game have a "no-no" word. The guest loses their pins when they say "wedding" or "bride" or whatever word you want to chose. Just make sure to keep it to one word, simple games have the best chance of success.

Trivia

"Who Knows the Bride Best" trivia can be a great way to show off your knowledge of the bride or (in the case of future mother-in-laws-to-be) get to know the bride better. Create a questionnaire of personal questions about the bride. You can include things like, "what was the bride's favorite movie growing up?" or "What's her favorite color/flower/etc.?" And things about the bride and groom like, "Where did they first meet?" or "How did he propose?" Keep it to about 20 questions and try to steer clear of questions that can be embarrassing in front of Great Aunt Ida.

Beware! Sometimes a question that you think is innocent, isn't. For example, I had on a trivia, "How did the groom propose?" and didn't clear that question with the bride first. At the shower the bride hemmed and hawed in front of the whole group that she didn't remember rather than admit that he had proposed after a romp in the sack! Oops! Clear your questions with the bride a week or two in advance of the party.

Hint! Have enough pens and pencils for all of the guests to participate!

Memories and/or Roast

A memory or roast event takes preparation but is completely worth it if your bride is the sentimental type. How do you know if your bride is the sentimental type? She's the friend with the scrapbooks of cheesy high school memories and puts the Christmas ornaments she made in kindergarten on the tree every year.

So for a memory or roast event at the party, you ask that every guest bring a picture or a memento of the bride as you've gotten to know her. Something you did together or saw her accomplish on her own. Ask the guests to be ready to share this memory with the group and write it down for the scrapbook. It's surprising what comes out in these memories, old Halloween photos, homemade hats that a bride made to cheer up her friend years before, baby pictures, etc. At the end of the party you have a memory from each guest to place in a scrapbook for the bride, who will treasure it because she's a sentimental gal.

To make this work you need to let your guests know in advance. On the invitations, preferably, then remind them when they RSVP and then remind them again the weekend before (everyone feels bad if they don't bring what they are supposed to).

The above describes a memory sharing sort of event. When a memory event turns ugly (and it does), it's called a roast. This can be super embarrassing and sometimes mean-spirited, depending on who is doing the roasting. Some brides can take it, some can't. My advice here is to try to stick to the safe ground above, unless your bride is the coolest chick you've ever met in your whole life.

Recipes

Like the memory sharing event, the recipe sharing needs organization as well. The basic idea is that your bride might run out of ideas in the kitchen, so her friends share their favorite recipes with her. You send out the recipe cards with the invitations and remind the guests a week before to bring them to the party (otherwise they forget). Ask each guest to share what they picked and why (good stories come out "the bride ate so much of this when she was little she got sick" or "My husband proposed a second time when he ate this"). It can be a good little icebreaker for the group.

Say Yes to the TP Dress

The Toilet Paper Dress is a staple of most bridal showers. The guests are broken up into groups. Each group has a model and the rest of the group designs a wedding dress made of toilet paper. Set a time limit of 5 or 10 minutes and see what creative results come out! The bride chooses the winning team. Usually you need to have 3-5 people on each team, so the number of teams depends on how many guests will be there. This one is great to pump energy back into a lull in the party, as everyone is on a team and gets to move about. Make sure you get a bulk package of toilet paper because each team will use several rolls!

Nice Touches

Favors

I would have forgotten favors all together at my first bridal shower if my mother had not reminded me! Favors are a way to say thank you to the guests and give them a small commemoration of the day. Favors don't necessarily need to be expensive, just thoughtful. I've been to showers that gave out homemade cookies and candies in customized boxes. The tea party I mentioned earlier in this chapter had small spoon holders as the favor. The favors for a spring themed bridal shower had small pots with packets of seeds in them. Before you decide what to do for a favor, think about the size of your party. If you have 20 guests and want to spend $5 per person on favors, you are looking at $100. Keep it small and thoughtful, you don't have to go overboard to make this a nice touch.

Flowers

Flowers are a great touch at a bridal shower. They have a spark of life and make it look like you really put a lot of thought into the entire event. I tend to get a mixed bouquet and break the bouquet into small flower vases. If you are on a budget, think about asking a neighbor if you can raid their rose bushes. Flowers live and die so quickly that they will likely be willing to share the gift and contribute in a small way to the celebration as well.

Gift Table

Let's face it. The bride is going to make out like a fiend at this party. Weddings make women sentimental and that makes them open their wallets! So when all of those packages come marching in the door, what are you going to do with them? A gift table unburdens the gifters of having to carry them around the party or trying to stash a large bundle under their chair with their purses. A gift table also creates a natural gathering point that everyone will congregate later in the party to watch the bride open her loot.

Presentation

Tiny touches can make a big impression. Like table cloths. If you want an extra gold star, shove a shoebox or two under the tablecloth to create raised tiers for the some of the food dishes. It creates the illusion that the food was possibly catered and makes for good pictures.

Gifts

When gift time rolls around it usually is close to the end of the party. The guests gather around the bride and watch her unwrap her bounty. Mostly it's gifts from the registry, but some guests will go off book in surprising and fun ways.

There are two jobs during the gift opening part of the bridal shower. The first is just making sure that the gifts are in arm-reach of the bride. Usually a kid at the party will volunteer to do this. If not, assign a bridesmaid.

The second job is to take notes of who gave which gift to your bride. The bride is expected to send thank you notes to each guest that lists specifically what was given to her by said guest. There's no way she's going to remember all of that, so it's up to you to write down it all down. Just draw a line down the paper. Left side who, right side what. Draw a line underneath it and start again. If you write slowly, you'll be okay because the bride will pause to read each card.

This IS your gift.

You are not expected to give the bride a gift. You are throwing this party for her. Your gift is done. Congrats.

……….. You're still there, huh? Feels a little awkward not to give a gift? Well, fine. If you insist on giving the bride a gift, make it something small, thoughtful and sentimental.

Tacky Behavior

Apparently some bridal showers have asked the guests to fill out an envelope with their own name and address. They then throw all the envelopes into a hat and draw a "winner." The idea is that the bride is SO BUSY that she can't write all the thank you notes AND be expected to address them. So basically the guest is addressing her own thank you note.

Uh. No.

These people have come and spent their time and money on the bride. She's expected to express her gratitude for it. The dentist asks you to fill out your own reminder cards. Asking the guests to address their own thank you notes says: "while you made time for me, I'm just too busy for you," and is just tacky.

When in Doubt

- ♥ Have champagne on hand and offer a toast.
- ♥ Have entertaining games or activities planned.
- ♥ Make sure there are enough chairs, cups, plates, etc.
- ♥ Delegate wherever possible.

Bachelorette Party

The bachelorette party is everything that the bridal shower is not. Where the bridal shower is classy, the bachelorette party can break loose and get raunchy. It's a bunch of girls hitting the town, looking to have a good time. Sequined clothes and dark makeup, alcoholic beverages and penis straws are all part of the fun and games. Bachelorette parties usually happen a week or two before the wedding, but under no circumstances should it be planned for the night before the wedding. A hungover bride will make everyone around her miserable on her big day - and she will make sure everyone knows it's your fault.

The success of any bachelorette party is to communicate with your bride. What does she expect? What does she not want? And how far can you push those limits that she will have fun without going over the edge?

Hint: most brides draw the line at strippers. That's usually a line to respect.

To have a fun bachelorette party doesn't require much. You don't need to go to Las Vegas to have a good time. Actually, I would discourage anyone from doing the Vegas weekend for the bachelorette party because it's too much pressure to spend money, have an over-the-top time and usually ends up with all the guests hating each other by the time you board the plane to go home. A good bar, or a strip of bars with live bands or DJs will be as good of a venue as any to have a great time.

The DO NOT Invite List

Let me say this once. It doesn't matter how cool Mom, Grandma or Great Aunt Ida are, they ARE NOT INVITED to the bachelorette party. EVER. I don't care if their picture is next to the word "fun" in the dictionary. No one else is going to be able to relax and let loose if a parental-unit is around.

Also on the DO NOT invite list are the groom, any ex-boyfriends or old crushes. Especially not all of the above. The bachelorette party is about the girls going out to blow off some steam. They can't do that if the bride and groom are so co-dependent that they can't spend a night apart. And inviting ex-boyfriends and old crushes - you know you are just trying to stir up drama, don't you? Well unless you are on a reality TV show and are desperate for ratings, don't do it.

If, by chance, you invite all of the above people and the bride ends her night crying in a bathroom stall, it's your job to get her out and rescue her. If she vomits on you, you deserve it.

Invitations

Invitations don't need to be quite as formal as the bridal shower. E-vites or another online invitation sites will do. Be sure to include where, when and any special instructions on the invitations. If the bachelorette party is not going to be eating at the venue, include that information in the invite, because drinking on an empty stomach could end the night early for some guests. Like the bridal shower, invites to the bachelorette party need to go out about a month in advance so that the guests can clear their calendar.

Themes/Games

There doesn't usually need to be a "theme" for going out on a Friday night, but games can be not only a great icebreaker, but can also bond the group for the night ahead. The best place to look for game ideas (and decorations, party favors, etc.) is at the adult store. Some areas call it the "adult bookstore" some just have XXX written on the side. Yeah, that place. Go check it out in daylight hours on a weekday - they are usually pretty clean.

Typically these places have clothes, toys and naughty knick-knacks. It's the knick-knack section that you'll end up doing the party shopping in. Usually

When Cool-Mom Gets Wasted.

Oh, it was an awkward night. The Mother-of-the-Bride was there. And the Mother-of-the-Groom. The sister of the groom was there too and horrified that the table was decorated in colorful penises. Because she was sitting next to her mom. It dawned on the mother-of-the-bride that her baby was getting married and wow, there's a lot of alcohol available at the bar!

By the middle of the night, the "cool mom" would point at the bride's breasts and yell "I MADE THAT!" loud enough for everyone to hear over the band. By the end of the night, "cool mom" couldn't understand why her daughter was mad at her and the groom's mom was "such a drag" because she left early. The bride was hiding in the bathroom, sobbing, and the bridesmaids were taking turns between distracting "cool mom" and shoving tissues under the bathroom door to the bride. No one had a fun time at this bachelorette party, except, perhaps, "cool mom."

there are bachelor and bachelorette decorations, an assortment of games and even wrapping paper in this area.

My favorite game is a sort of Bingo/Scavenger Hunt. The tasks are on a scratch off card (like the lotto) and the tasks are things like "pee in the men's room" or "convince a guy to give you his wallet condom." The entire party competes to finish the first item to win a prize and have the privilege of scratching off the next task to-do. The prizes come from the knick-knack section too, so people get weird tasting sex crèmes and penis suckers for their efforts. And they love them. I'm not kidding, they probably never use them, but they love opening them and screaming and laughing and showing everyone else at the party.

It's all about bonding and girl time. Other things that work well are penis straws (you give them out at the beginning of the night and carry them with you from bar to bar), a decorative veil for the bride (which usually will get the whole group free cover and a few free drinks), and pin the penis on the male pin-up poster (if the bar isn't too crowded). Try to create situations where everyone is laughing and enjoying the adventure together.

If drinking is off the table

Whether it's due to age, religion, or addiction, maybe alcohol is not an option for your party. That's okay. The bachelorette party is still about bonding and girl time. Comedy clubs usually have an 18-and-up age limit. Dave and Buster's have party packages. There are even pole dancing classes for bachelorette parties. Bowling, mini-golfing, go-karting, are all ways to let loose and have a little fun. The whole point of a bachelorette party is to go out with your best girlfriends, laugh uncontrollably and make some memories. You'll have to be a little more creative than the traditional route, but you can do it.

Strippers

To strip or not to strip, that is the question. Not you personally, of course, but to hire one. The answer is: it depends. You've got to ask the bride about this one. Quite a few couples have a "no stripper" rule with their partners. That should be respected. If the bride is really uncomfortable with the idea, that also should be respected because the party is for her to have fun, not for the rest of the party to have fun at her expense.

When to push the limit.

"I don't want to get drunk," said the control-freak bride. I said, "Uh-huh, okay." Then I proceeded to include the following instructions on all of the invitations, "While we all love the bride and want her to have fun, she will probably stop drinking the moment one of us says 'Let's get drunk!' However, if we just keep a free drink in her hand all night, I think she'll have a great time!"

It was a blurry night for everyone in attendance. As the bride was lying on the bathroom floor the morning after the party, she told me, "Best Party... EVER."

Mission accomplished.

On the other hand, some women think that strippers are great! If that's the case, figure out if you want to do a house party or go out to an actual strip club. Call up a few; you'll usually get a choice of firemen, construction worker, policeman, etc. Find out the rates and see who is willing to split the costs. If there is a "male revue" coming through town, it might be more economical to go to that way. Larger groups can also be more fun because it makes it okay to scream and clap with a crowd. Either way you go, be sure to put a warning on the invitations. Guests need their notice to bring one-dollar bills!

What happens in...

We live in a social media world. The temptation to click, tag and post is enormous. But what happens in Vegas stays on YouTube. Forever.

Part of all that bonding I was talking about earlier should include a pact. A girl's code, we-never-tell-anyone-about-this agreement whether the party gets wild or not. Because what's tame for you might be wild for another guest and you talking about it online or to your friends might bring her some embarrassment. Not telling anyone else leads to winks over the rehearsal dinner and nicknames that your respective spouses are still mystified about years later. A shared secret is much more special than a cheap post on Facebook.

When in Doubt

- ♥ Invite the bride's friends.
- ♥ Don't load the party with your own friend's because they're "funner."
- ♥ Chat up random guys at the bar.
- ♥ Bring a flask; sneaking something naughty in the ladies room can be a laugh.
- ♥ Play games, challenges or truth or dare.

Odd Facts:

The bridesmaid dress can sometimes be flattering. Pippa Middleton became an overnight global sensation after wearing a figure-hugging ivory bridesmaid dress at Prince William and Kate Middleton's wedding in 2011. Pippa was inundated with offers ranging from speaking engagements to endorsement deals for clothing, fragrances and the travel industry. She was even offered $5 million dollars to film a sex tape!

Chapter 5
Biting Your Tongue

If you are someone who takes pride in always saying what you mean, tweeting your every thought or just speaking your truth as loudly as possible, this section might be hard for you. If it is hard for you, it probably is all that much more important that you read it and try to abide by it. For the sake of the bride and your own long-term sanity, sometimes you'll just have to bite your tongue.

Dresses Not Fitting

You've ordered your dress, you've gone in for your fitting... and the dress is horribly miss-cut. Your first inclination may be to text the bride from the dressing room "OMG my dressed is screwed up!" But there are some things that the bride need never know.

The bride might be your best friend and the person you would normally turn to in these sorts of crises, but this is not the time. The wedding is fast approaching and the bride has her own mini fires to put out. Don't dump gasoline on her fires because you want to commiserate about yours.

By chance, if the dress comes in the wrong size, color or cut, there should be time for an emergency re-order. Most of those big warehouse stores have that option. If the time constraint is too short, there's also eBay and other websites that specialize in bridesmaid dresses. You may be able to find the exact same dress, just slightly used - not ideal, but will work in a pinch.

In that moment of panic in the dressing room, call another bridesmaid. One that will be discreet and not turn around and call the bride. If dresses start coming in wrong, all the bridesmaids need to be warned regardless, so they can get their fittings done and, if necessary, reorder as soon as possible.

Outrageous Demands

There were a lot of outrageous demands in chapter one, Sidebar "When to Run" but what if it's not so clear-cut? The bride has so many friends, she asks for two bridal showers instead of one. She asks for your help creating guests gifts, and leaves you to do the lion's share. She demands that your hair be done a certain way on her wedding day. What is reasonable and when is it okay to say no?

First of all, if you ever feel uncomfortable when you are being asked to do something, that's a pretty good indicator that you should say no. Politely.

When what you are being asked to do isn't something you can say no to, try to work towards the middle ground. If she has so many friends that she needs two bridal showers, maybe the bridesmaids should split the responsibility of two showers between them.

If the bride is unwilling to budge, go recruiting. She's asking all of her friends to go to Mexico for three-days. Surely not everyone will be going, there's gotta be some of her friends that think a pub-crawl will suffice. Brainstorm together for how best to approach the bride. There's power in numbers, use them!

As for the hair-do's (make up, etc.)... consult the hairdresser. She (or he!) is the expert on hair and what it will and will not do. Getting three women's hair to look the same is pretty near impossible and the bride will often take a "no" from an expert when a no from you won't do.

Cold Feet

Did you ever have that really awkward experience in high school, when a friend is having trouble with her boyfriend and you jump in and tell her that he's not good enough, he's a scumbag, blah, blah, blah, only for them to get back together a week later and suddenly your friend is mad at you?

Yeah. Don't go there if the bride has cold feet. This is an incredibly stressful time in the bride's life. She's making a decision about who she wants to be with for the rest of her life. Some people need to take a breather and ask themselves "is this really what I want?" It's okay, it's normal.

The very best thing you can do for her, as a friend, is to be there to listen and ask questions. Some people need to hear their own thoughts and fears out loud before they can really process what's going on. So listen to

Bargain Shopping Mother-of-the-Bride

I had to remind myself that she was "helping" or at least attempting to, when the mother-of-the-bride showed up at my door with her garage sale finds.

"These would make great decorations! And look! It says 50 cents but I got it for a quarter!"

Her proud bargain was a horrid collection of paper bridal decorations that looked like they had been in storage since the 1950's. The white was turning yellow and the water stains made them bend in weird ways.

"Uh, thanks," I stammered. "I'll see where I can use them." Diplomatically, one decoration did make it to a table, in a room that no one would go into. The rest were returned with apologies after the shower.

what she is saying and ask clarifying questions for her to get things straight in her own mind. She'll make the decisions from there. Make sure that she knows that you love her and will support her decision no matter what. That's what friends are for!

Unhelpful Bridesmaids

Perhaps there is a bridesmaid in the crew that doesn't actually want to be there. This may be a spiteful sister or a soon-to-be stepdaughter who is only there because she has to be. She refuses to pay her share. She makes every decision a chore with unhelpful comments. She is a black cloud at every occasion. She is not supportive of the marriage.

Unfortunately, you can't ask the bride to kick the bitch to the curb. What you can do is speak directly to the sour-faced bridesmaid in question. Try to work with her budget if it is strictly a financial concern. If she will not budge, you can make clear that if she will not be helping host the party, that it will be made apparent to all guests that she is not a part of it, including having her name taken off the invitations.

If the sour-faced bridesmaid is undermining in other ways (snide comments, bad advice or negativity), it's time to pull her aside and have another kind of conversation. This one is a "why do you want to be here?" talk. Listen to what her replies are. Clarify if she is there to support her bride and then ask her how her behavior has been helpful or hurtful. Reiterate that being a bridesmaid is about seeing the bride through a stressful-chaotic time, and if she isn't here to support, it would be better to leave than to poison the wedding with her toxicity. Don't expect a miracle, but she might put a better face on it from there.

Distraction and/or Temporary Amnesia

Being a bridesmaid, out of the goodness of your heart can sometimes be taken for granted by the bride. Sometimes the bride gets an overblown sense of entitlement. Sometimes her wedding takes over your life too. Let me reassure you, you are entitled to set limits and have a life too.

If you are at the end of your rope, maybe it's time to hang up the taffeta dress for a bit, put the phone on silent and do something just for you. Like watch Bridezilla's and comfort yourself that at least your bride didn't do "that." Open a bottle of wine. Drink with a straw until temporary amnesia kicks in. It's okay, I won't tell.

When in Doubt
- ♥ Try to be diplomatic.
- ♥ Choose your battles.

Odd Facts
Did you know that there's a Guinness World Record for the most bridesmaids in a wedding? In 2010, an Ohio bride broke the record with 110 bridesmaids in her wedding. Each bridesmaid was asked to chose their own dress in either purple or teal and each bridesmaid carried a single rose.

Chapter 6
The Essential Checklists

Note: These timelines are for <u>very</u> organized women. See the Appendix for what my typical timeline looks like.

Bridal Shower

3+ Months Before

- ✓ Get the bride's input. Some girls dream about every aspect of their wedding, some have no idea. The bridesmaids will make most of the decisions about the bridal shower but you can try to incorporate some of her ideas to make it special.
- ✓ Call or meet with all of the bridesmaids to set a budget for the shower.
- ✓ Set the date. Ideally the shower will be 1-2 months prior to the wedding. However, if there are family and friends coming in from out-of-area it might make sense to do it several days before the wedding.
- ✓ If the bridal shower is going to take place at a restaurant or public venue, make reservations now.
- ✓ Confer with the bride for a guest list. You will need physical addresses for invitations. If the list is long remind the bride that etiquette dictates guests at the bridal shower be invited to the wedding.

2 Months Before

- ✓ Call important guests (mother-of-the-bride, mother-of-the-groom, Great Aunt Ida) and ask them to save the date.
- ✓ Buy bridal shower invitations.
- ✓ Remind the bride that you need addresses for the invitations.
- ✓ Make a detailed to-do list and delegate among the bridesmaids.

1 Month Before

- ✓ Assemble and address invitations. Don't forget information about the couple's registries. If it's a theme party, make sure to provide proper gift-giving instructions.
- ✓ Mail invitations. (Ask at the post office for romantic or flowery stamps, they are nice touch compared to the standard liberty statue or flag stamps.)
- ✓ Make final decisions about decorations, menu, favors, music, and games.
- ✓ Order special cake from the bakery.
- ✓ Shop for decorations, paper goods, and game materials.
- ✓ Purchase favors.
- ✓ Remind bridesmaids of what they have committed to (bringing a dish or decorations).

2+ Weeks Before

- ✓ Make a shopping list for the food and drinks. Scope out where to buy any hard-to-find ingredients.
- ✓ Purchase alcohol and mixers, if you're having cocktails.
- ✓ Order flowers.
- ✓ Burn a playlist for background music at the shower.
- ✓ 1 Week Before
- ✓ Confirm reservations (if applicable).

- ✓ Confirm orders and delivery/pickup times.
- ✓ Call and confirm RSVPs.
- ✓ Pick up any decorations or serving ware being lent to you by friends or neighbors.
- ✓ Wrap party favors and prizes.
- ✓ Buy groceries.
- ✓ Prep shower games and activities.

1 Day Before

- ✓ Prepare any menu items that won't get soggy overnight. Prep everything that will need to be assembled the next day.
- ✓ Decorate.
- ✓ Text the bridesmaids and let them know when you need them the next day.
- ✓ Run last-minute errands.

Bachelorette Party

3+ Months Before

- ✓ Ask the bride what she wants (or doesn't want) in terms of a bachelorette party.
- ✓ Establish her comfort levels. Find out what is off the table and what isn't. Remember, you want her to cut loose; you don't want her to run screaming.
- ✓ Set a date. Ideally this will be a Friday or Saturday night two to three weeks before the wedding.
- ✓ Create the guest list.

2 Months Before

- ✓ Call the other bridesmaids and brainstorm ideas for venues, games and activities. Keep as many details as possible a surprise for the bride.
- ✓ Decide on a venue and, if appropriate, make reservations.
- ✓ If the party is going to be "on the move" consider booking a chauffeured limo, bus, or van for the evening. Get quotes and compare rates.
- ✓ Send out a "save the date" email to the guests.
- ✓ Research and book any "entertainment" that might make an appearance at the party.

1 Month Before

- ✓ Email invitations. Texting is okay too. Give guests a head's up if there is a cost involved (the Aussie Thunder From Down Under tickets aren't free, you know).
- ✓ Devise an itinerary if you are doing a pub-crawl or like. Make sure the party starts at a restaurant; binge drinking on an empty stomach is a sure way to end the night early! Pick a restaurant that's fun, noisy and a bit rowdy to set the tone for the night.

✓ To book your transportation for the proper length of time, you are going to have to scope out how long you will want to stay at each bar. Call bars to see if there are bachelorette freebies and specials. If applicable, make bar reservations too.

✓ Make your transportation reservation(s). Keep in mind that if it is prom season or summer season, limos tend to book-up early.

1 Week Before

✓ Go to an adult store and buy bachelorette party accessories such as the novelty veil, penis straws, and any party favors.

✓ Make a list of the games you want to play, with rules or you might forget!

✓ Confirm RSVPs.

✓ Confirm all reservations.

1 Day Before

✓ Let the bride know the general plan for the night. It's okay to keep some of the details a surprise!

✓ Text the guests the meeting place and time, and if the party is moving to another location, text that too. Someone always runs behind!

✓ Re-confirm all reservations.

✓ Hydrate.

✓ Get plenty of sleep.

Wedding Day

Note: This schedule presumes a 12-month engagement. Should you be looking at a tighter schedule, this can be adjusted as needed.

Once you've agreed to be a bridesmaid...

- ✓ Send a congratulations/engagement card to bride and groom (it will mostly likely end up in her scrapbook).
- ✓ Buy engagement gift and, if applicable, attend the engagement party.
- ✓ Offer to help the bride look at dresses, venues for ceremony and reception.
- ✓ 8-10 Months Before
- ✓ Set up an informal get-together of bridesmaids, with the bride of course!
- ✓ Attend wedding shows and expos with the bride.
- ✓ Accompany bride for wedding dress and bridesmaid dress shopping.
- ✓ 6-8 Months Before
- ✓ If the bridesmaid dress is not available for you to try on, get professional measurements taken by a seamstress.
- ✓ Order your bridesmaid dress. If it comes from a "David's Bridal" type store, you can walk in and order. Otherwise a bridesmaid might be in charge of collecting and placing orders.
- ✓ Ask the bride about any accessories you need to purchase (shoes, jewelry, wraps).
- ✓ Begin planning bridal shower.

4-6 Months Before

- ✓ Ask the bride about making hotel accommodations.
- ✓ Offer to help bride stuff, address and puts stamps on invitations. Scope out what other projects are on the horizon and plan accordingly.

2-4 Months Before

- ✓ Throw the bridal shower.
- ✓ Begin planning the bachelorette party.
- ✓ Make appointment for the bridesmaid dress fitting (bring shoes and undergarments for the wedding to the dress fitting).

1-2 Months Before

- ✓ Make appointment for final bridesmaid's dress fitting (bring shoes and undergarments for the wedding).
- ✓ Offer to help the bride with wedding favors.
- ✓ Attend the bride's final fitting to learn the bustling for her dress.
- ✓ Buy wedding present for bride and groom and have it shipped to them.

3 Weeks Before

- ✓ Throw the bachelorette party.
- ✓ Start planning a toast for rehearsal dinner and/or reception.
- ✓ Offer to help bride with any last minute projects.
- ✓ 2 Weeks Before
- ✓ Prepare the Day-of Emergency Kit.
- ✓ Pick up bridesmaids dress after final alterations.
- ✓ Take a walk in your party shoes to scuff up the bottom. If they hurt right away, this is your chance to either get new shoes or blister patches.
- ✓ Do any haircut, styling or coloring of your hair.

1 Week Before

- ✓ Gather items to pack for wedding.
- ✓ Practice toast(s) for the rehearsal dinner and/or reception.
- ✓ Coordinate with bride and let the other bridesmaids know when/ where to meet for rehearsal.
- ✓ Organize snacks for the primping room.

✓   If applicable, eyebrow waxing and/or spray tan.

2 Days Before

✓   Wrestle the to-do list away from the bride. Divvy it up between bridesmaids and knock it out.

✓   Pull cash from the ATM. Keep in mind no-host bars, professional make-up and hairstylists as well as the "money dance" and any random taxis you might need to escape into.

1 Day Before:

✓   Show up early for the rehearsal.

✓   Attend the rehearsal dinner.

✓   Keep the bride company the night before her big day. Bring Valium, if necessary.

Check the Website!

Many brides are opting to create a website for guests and attendants to reference leading up to the big day. Directions, times and other important details are listed here as well as cute pictures and stories about the happy couple.

The bride has put an incredible effort into the creation of the website. She is also incredibly overwhelmed and sensitive. You may think, "But I'm her best friend, we are going to talk anyway, why shouldn't I just ask her what time I need to be there?"

Because you are in the wedding and can't look at a goddamn website that she poured her soul into, that's why. Or at least that's how she is going to see it once all of her attendants and guests ask her the details that are readily available on the website.

Save your head from being bitten off. Check the website, compliment it, and then ask any questions you may still have.

Day of Wedding Kit

Every wedding has a mini-disaster. There are so many details that go into the day; it's virtually guaranteed that something will go wrong. Take this tote bag of essentials with you from where you are primping to just before you walk down the aisle. Delegate a friend to stash it underneath your table at the reception while you are getting your pictures taken. You'll be the lifesaver of the party!

Essentials

For Clothing
- ✓ Sewing kit with needles, thread, and buttons
- ✓ Toupee tape (Not what you are thinking. It keeps clothes in place.)
- ✓ Scissors
- ✓ Stick-on instant hemming tape
- ✓ Clear nail polish (for runs)
- ✓ White chalk (for covering stains)
- ✓ Extra panty hose
- ✓ Safety pins
- ✓ Spot remover (the instant no-wash kind)
- ✓ Static-cling spray

From the Medicine Cabinet
- ✓ Aspirin (or pain reliever of choice)
- ✓ Band-Aids
- ✓ Dental floss/toothpicks
- ✓ Eye drops
- ✓ Hand towelettes
- ✓ Tampons/sanitary napkins
- ✓ Blister protection
- ✓ Contact case and solution
- ✓ For Beauty

- ✓ Extra earring backs
- ✓ Hair pins/ponytail holder
- ✓ Breath mints/spray
- ✓ Tissues
- ✓ Tweezers
- ✓ Sunscreen
- ✓ Comb/brush
- ✓ Hair spray
- ✓ Makeup (for touch-ups)
- ✓ Mirror
- ✓ Nail file

And because you never know:
- ✓ Krazy Glue
- ✓ Credit Card
- ✓ Cellular phone

Shoe Stretching Techniques

It's the eleventh hour and the shoes you were required to wear don't fit right. What to do?

If you find that your shoes are too tight, this technique works for most shoe types. Put on two pairs of socks (or one thick pair) and wet the socks where the shoes pinch the most. Next, put on your shoes. Using a hair dryer, apply high heat to the areas that are most uncomfortable for about two minutes. Walk around until the shoes are comfortable or until the socks are dry.

Too lose? No blister pad handy? A panty liner can quickly be trimmed to fit at the back of the heel. It even has its own self-adhesive strip!

Chapter 7
Etiquette

You've prepped the party, you've bought the dress. It's time to tackle how you are expected to act. We aren't going to go over crossing legs and all of the Miss Manners tips on table decorum. This chapter is more of a survival guide on how to get through the pomp and circumstance without putting your foot in it.

Hostess with the Mostest

You've sent out the invitations and laid out the cheese spread. Guests are knocking any moment. So what is expected of you at this event? Although the party is for the benefit of the bride, you are hosting it. A good hostess makes guests feel welcome. You compliment the guest's dress, ask to take their coat, and let them know where the bathroom is. You fill cups and make small talk.

A good hostess compliments the wrapping on the guest's gifts. When the gifts are opened, you ooh and aah like everyone else. You do not ask how much a gift cost. If you really want it for yourself, you can ask where it came from and then check it out after the party is over. You also do not talk about how much throwing the party cost you. That makes guests feel uncomfortable.

Their Behavior

Guests are expected to be polite. They are expected to dote on the bride, carry on conversations and participate in games. A bridal shower guest is expected to bring a gift and congratulate the bride. They are expected to compliment the venue and your cheese spread. If the guests aren't doing these things, take a beat to figure out if they A.) don't know anyone and are shy, B.) are so wrapped up in themselves that they can't be bothered to be nice or C.) aren't supportive of the wedding.

Fortunately, A and B are easily handled. For a shy person, start bringing guests over to introduce. Usually one will ask the other, "How do you know the bride?" and a conversation is started from there. For the self-absorbed guest, when it comes to game time, you can ask that everyone put their cellphones away to participate.

The Do-It-Yourself-Er

Weddings are expensive. You know this because it isn't even your wedding and you're already out several hundred dollars. Brides frequently look for ways to cut costs and often over-estimate what can be accomplished the day before the wedding. I think if it was possible to play their own music and take their own pictures, they would. I've seen brides playing DJ and brides scrambling to bake their own cake. I've seen brides breakdown the day before the wedding because the favors still need to be put together and the venue decorated and, and, and...

As your bride is discussing doing these crazy things with you, encourage her to spend where it makes sense. Also point out how stressful the day and the day before are going to be if she doesn't delegate and complete as much as possible leading up to the day before the wedding. Remind her that friends and family are going to be flying in before the wedding and wouldn't it be more comfortable spending time with them rather than running around doing all those last minute errands? If she starts to have a melt down have her make a list and delegate it for her.

She probably will bend to the peer pressure of everyone at the party doing the same. If she doesn't that's on her, not you.

If one of the guests is not behaving appropriately because they don't approve of the wedding, the best you can do is ignore the bitch. If she's making inappropriate comments to get a response, don't rise to the bait. It's between her and the bride, it's not your place to defend or get in a fight about it. Don't let her ruin the party. Just strike her name from the bachelorette party list and move on.

Timeliness.

If you are someone who is always on time, good for you. We all admire your abilities to be where you need to be, when you need to be there. For some of us, being on time is a bit of a challenge. For example, the very first wedding I was a bridesmaid in, I was 15 minutes late to the rehearsal. Maybe 20. For someone who is chronically late, this seemed like no big deal to me. Until I saw the relief on the bride's face when I walked through the door. I think she might have been freaking out that I wasn't going to come at all. That maybe I had decided to boycott the wedding!

Then the other bridesmaids looked at me like I was an idiot. The mother of the bride asked me some very pointed questions about why I was late. Even the priest gave me one of those "You've done wrong" looks that priests are so good at and I had nothing to defend myself with. I was just late.

Make your life and everyone else's life easier. For all events, plan on being there 15 minutes early. Just write down the start time 15 minutes earlier than it is and try to stick to it. Being on time takes the stress off the bride and the target off of you so the whole event can go much more smoothly.

Connectivity

Have you ever heard the term "be in the moment?" Like the example of the bridal shower guest earlier in this chapter, it's incredibly rude to show up to someone else's party and spend the entire time wrapped up in your phone. You are attending the party so that everyone can have this moment to be together for the bride. Obsessive cell phone usage is not "in the moment" and rather says "I'm physically here because I agreed to be, but I'm bored and would much rather be somewhere else."

Texting should be a means of communicating, "Where the hell are you? We started 15 minutes ago," to the other bridesmaids that are late. (But not you. You read this book and are on time.) Texting is also for last minute directions to guests on how to get to a party/shower. Texting is NOT for talking with your boyfriend or friends about whatever is going on in your life. Be in the moment. Enjoy the moment.

Don't Steal!

Not that I think that you would. But some stories are too good not to share! The bride and groom placed a wish bowl in the front lobby of the venue and seeded it with $100. Guests were asked to place wishes, words of wisdom or money into the bowl throughout the festivities.

At the end of the reception the bride and groom contacted security when they found only $80 in the bowl! Security camera footage was reviewed and found a surprising culprit... the maid of honor! Security informed the bride of who had the money and where she had hidden it. The bride opted to handle the theft directly with the maid of honor.... can you say awkward?

Social Media

Everyone knows where you are at all times because you are obsessed with checking in on Facebook. Or you tweet your activities hourly. Your friends understand this because they are your friends and followers and see it all of the time. They expect it of you. However, the friends of the bride just met you and have friended you instantly on Facebook. Before you start tagging and posting and checking them in, you need to step back a moment.

Tagging and checking in friends who do not want their lives shared to that extent online can cause problems. Perhaps she is Facebook friends with her boss, co-workers and grandmother. Maybe you shouldn't just presume it's okay to check your new friend in at the bar and tag the picture of her puking back at the hotel. It's funny at the time, and you might assume your new friend is smart enough to have Facebook locked down, but those security settings are changed with alarming frequency and sometimes posts slip through the cracks.

Wing Man

You are the bride's wingman. Leading up to the wedding, you are the one she calls. Check out venues, okay. Bridal expo, sure. Cake tasting appointment, count me in! As the wedding gets closer, the chores become less fun and more frantic. Especially if your bride is disorganized and doesn't ask for help (See: The Do-It-Yourself-er).

Communication is key to helping a bride to the altar. Let her know when you are available and that you are willing to help. That said, you need to make sure that you clear time in your calendar to help! Block out the weekend before the wedding. Also plan on being at her beck and call the two days leading up to the wedding. If the bride says she's working up until the day before the wedding, say "uh-huh" and clear the decks. She's going to end up having the mother of all pre-wedding meltdowns the day before. Be prepared to call in "sick" to spend the day talking her off the ledge and doing last minute errands like ring polishing. Because that ring needs to sparkle.

All that said, make sure you schedule some "me" time too. The last few months have been all about her. Especially if the bride is your sister, plan some things for yourself so the sister-jealousy monster doesn't rear its ugly head. Balance is the way to keep your sanity. Make sure you get your exercise and friend time and do whatever it is that relaxes you.

Wedding

Have you ever stood up in front of a crowd of people and had them stare at you? Were you uncomfortable? People who are uncomfortable tend to fidget. Scratch themselves, shift their feet, play with the bouquet of flowers in their hands... this can be very distracting to the guests!

Take a deep breath and remind yourself that everyone is staring at the bride and groom, not you. Try to pay attention to the ceremony. Sometimes you can catch sweet little moments whispered between the bride and groom at the altar. Smile and try to look serene.

Pictures

Immediately after the bride and groom say their "I do's" the entire

If You Get Sick

No one wants to be sick for an event you have helped plan... but sometimes an illness knocks you flat! Should you come down with the flu, migraine or some other illness, you gotta be willing to show up to the events that you can.

Start drinking fluids, taking whatever medications will relieve the symptoms and assess the damage. Prioritize the wedding ceremony first and try to hold it together through the pictures. If you have to duck out of the wedding reception early and skip the rehearsal dinner altogether, you may have to apologize, but she will forgive you.

As much as possible, try to avoid touching the bride and groom (they don't want to be sick on the honeymoon) as well as the very young and the elderly.

wedding party is swept off to take pictures together. Touch up makeup if there is time; otherwise get straight to the smiling! Wait! The bride's train needs to be straightened. The flower girl isn't looking at the camera. The groomsmen have snuck off for a beer. The ring-bearer is hiding in the bushes.

Herd the cats that you can. Keep smiling. The entire wedding party has been sequestered all day getting ready and the wedding went off without a hitch. It seems like everyone is breathing for the first time all day! Do what you can to keep the pictures rolling. The sooner they are done the real party can begin!

Reception

Congrats! You made it to the party! You can finally relax and do nothing!

Uh. Sorry to break it to you BUT…

There are one hundred guests at the party. The bride is only one woman. There is no way she is going to be able to visit and charm each individual guest all night. You have gotten practice at being a hostess at the shower and bachelorette party. You are an emissary of the bride at the reception and mini-hostess for the guests. Work the table, work the room. You have probably met quite a few of the guests at this point and can start by checking in with the ones you recognize.

"Wasn't the ceremony beautiful?"
"Isn't the bride's dress fantastic?"
"How about this weather?"

You can work that room like a champ. Some guests will have questions like where is the bathroom? Who is watching the kids? When is the cake being cut? Make sure you are familiar enough with the venue and the schedule to answer the basic questions. Otherwise you have guests pestering the bride with small questions rather than visiting with her and doting on her.

Gift

How much is a bridesmaid expected to spend on a wedding gift? After all, you've already bought a dress, engagement gift, thrown several parties... how much is enough? Well, let me say first: Yes, you do need to give a gift. Second, the rule of thumb for wedding gifts is to at least "cover your head." The term comes from caterers who charge per person or "per head." So you need to give a gift that at least covers the cost of the meal the bride and groom is serving you at the reception. You can certainly give more if you want to.

Your Date

If you are already married, it's a given that your spouse is coming. For argument's sake, this section is going to assume that you aren't.

To bring a date or not to bring a date? Actually, this might be a decision made for you. If your invitation says your name and "guest" your bride is saying it's okay to bring a date. If it has your name and your name alone on the inside envelope, it's a no-go. Caterers charge per head and your bride isn't going to spring for your date. You can appeal directly, and sometimes if the RSVPs are low, then you can get your date added on later, but your date didn't make the A-list of invites.

But, let's say that the invitation does have "guest" listed. Before you invite your significant other, there are a few considerations to take into account. First, you are going to be very busy the day of the wedding, will be whisked away after the ceremony for pictures and then are expected to be leading the funky chicken on the dance floor. Does your date know enough of the guests to fend for himself and have a good time? Will your date be sulking and annoyed that you are not paying attention to him?

Second, does the reception have a table for the entire bridal party that you are expected to sit at? If so, you won't be sitting with your date, even at dinner. It could make for a very lonely day for your date.

Third, how serious is your relationship? Sometimes going to a wedding can put a lot of pressure on a couple. The internal pressure of "are we ever going to do this?" can destroy a relationship early. Ditto for the wedding guests that are so happy to see one couple married off that they start asking every couple in sight if they are altar bound. Is your relationship ready to face the grilling?

When in Doubt
- ♥ Be early to every event.
- ♥ Be prepared to make small talk.
- ♥ Put away the cellphone and be in the moment.
- ♥ Don't Steal!

Odd Fact
The term "best man" historically comes from Scotland where Scotsmen kidnapped their future brides. The friend of the groom who helped the most in the abduction was declared to be the best man.

Chapter 8
Leading Up to the Big Day

It's almost here! The day you've been waiting to celebrate has been sneaking up fast as while you weren't watching! Do yourself a favor and block sometime out in your calendar now for the week leading up to the event.

Errands

Whether they are yours or hers, errands are always a part of the wedding process. Errands can be anything from calling and confirming reservations to running all over town to find the perfect ribbon for her something blue because the one she has isn't quite the right shade. If your bride has a list, great! Divvy it up between the bridesmaids and knock what you can out. If your bride is not that organized, sit her down with a pen, paper, and if necessary, a bottle of wine and make her list out everything that needs to be done. There is nothing worse than saving all of your errands to the last minute and then having the bride's list dumped on you in the eleventh hour too.

While we are on the topic, write out your list too. Try to get your personal responsibilities taken care of the weekend or two before because starting a few days before the wedding the bride is probably going to fill your day for you.

Pampering and Prepping

You haven't forgotten about you, right? Plan out your personal care and book your appointments early. Haircuts, dying, straightening, perming, relaxing (add your hair regiment here) should take place two weeks prior to the wedding. Should a hair disaster befall you, two weeks will give you enough time to come up with a solution.

Waxing should never be done the day of the event and probably shouldn't be done the day before, either. The skin turns red for hours when the wax is pulled off and the possibility always exists to have some sort of allergic reaction to the wax. Try to knock this one out the weekend prior or early in the week leading up to the wedding.

Tanning usually takes several sessions to have a lasting effect. If you go in for your first session the day before the wedding, you are likely to overexpose and burn rather than tan. Plan several short sessions to get the tanned look you are hoping for and to avoid the burn and peel cycle. Should you spray tan instead of using a tanning bed, one visit should be all that you need but the spray tan appointment should still be done a few days in advance. Spray tans can take a few days to look natural and usually have a day or two of "sloughing off" where the tanning material literally flakes off your skin. The tanning material won't look good on your dress or the brides dress after you hug her!

Rehearsal Dinner

In a perfect world, the rehearsal dinner is a time to relax and bond the night before the wedding. It's an intimate gathering of the wedding party and family to break bread and raise a toast to the couple before the hoopla begins. There's usually toasting and sharing of embarrassing stories as well as in-laws getting to know each other better. Hopefully your rehearsal dinner will be idyllic and calm.

Unfortunately, the rehearsal dinner more often than not is an awkward chore that neither bride nor groom wants to attend. They usually are a bundle of raw nerves, brimming over with lists of last minute things to do and (possibly) cold feet. Added to that is family dynamics, possible confusion over who is paying the bill and Uncle Art displaying his alcoholic tendencies because, "Hey, we're going to be family tomorrow."

Note: Traditionally the groom's parents pay for the rehearsal dinner. Check with the bride if that is the case.

Your job, as always, is to do what you can to make the day go smoothly. Keep the bride calm and distracted. If something needs to be done, whether it is making small talk with the mother of the groom or having the bartender cut off Uncle Art, do it with gusto. Remind the bride that you pick your friends and your husband to be, but you can't choose family.

At the rehearsal dinner you are not expected to give a toast. If you've been procrastinating your speech for the wedding reception, this is a good opportunity to make note of what other people are saying and blatantly steal it.

Bring extra cash. No-host bar means that each guest pays for his or her own drink. On top of your own drinks, you might end up fetching drinks for the bride if it will take her stress level down a notch. It is also a good idea to have cash if there is a total breakdown over the bill and you need to cover your own meal (rare, but it happens). Note that I am suggesting cash and not card. Cash gives you the ability to throw money on the table and make a quick escape if you need to whisk the bride away from her own relatives.

When in Doubt
- ♥ Touch base with the bride and offer to help with her to do list.
- ♥ Finish your own personal errands the weekend before.
- ♥ Engage family members in small talk.
- ♥ Carry cash, just in case.

Odd Facts
The wedding tradition in Greece is to write the names of all the bride's unmarried female friends and relatives on the sole of her shoe. After the wedding, the shoe is examined and those whose names have been worn off are said to be next in line for a journey up the aisle.

Bridesmaid Saves the Day With Sunscreen!
The entire bridal party cares about how they look on the wedding day, hours and tons of money have been spent primping for that walk down the aisle. However, all of that gets thrown out the window as people scramble the day before the wedding.

Typically people comment how nice the weather is going to be for the wedding, and then completely ignore what that bright sunny day is doing to their skin. No one wants to be a lobster in the pictures and wine in pain dancing to the YMCA. Be the hero at the rehearsal dinner and slather the bride and bridesmaids with sunblock.

Chapter 9
Heading Down the Aisle

Aren't you excited? The big day is here! If the wedding takes place at night, you are lucky, you might get to sleep in. For most weddings, it is morning or afternoon ceremony and much pampering and prepping still needs to be done. An organized bride will have detailed timetables and schedules laid out. If you are the kind of girl that rolls out of bed, throws on a t-shirt and struts out the door, you need to understand is that everything is going to take longer than you would expect.

Hair / Makeup

There's the bride, the mother-of-the-bride, you and the bridesmaids as well as the flower girl. In all likelihood, there is only one makeup artist and hair stylist for you each to share. First, the bride has dibs. If she's ready, she's first in line. In fact, there is no line for her. The hairstylist and makeup artist might drop your prep halfway through in favor of getting the bride done when she is ready. It's her day.

Second, the mother-of-the-bride has higher priority than the bridesmaids and flower girl. She has to wait in line, but it's likely that all of her friends from the last 30 years are in the audience, plus she's probably helped foot the bill. Don't cut in front of the mother-of-the-bride because she's usually just as stressed as the bride and more likely to cut you!

Coordinate the order with the rest of the bridesmaids. Whoever isn't getting their hair or makeup done is usually curling the flower girl's hair. Don't stress, if you are at the back of the line. If push comes to shove and the time is too short, you've been doing your own hair and makeup since puberty, you can do it now too.

Bring Food

Prep starts at 10am, ceremony is at 2pm and dinner isn't until 5pm. How are you and the rest of the bridal party going to eat? Remarkably, most people forget this step and are seriously hungry and grouchy by the time the second round of photos come along. Do yourself and fellow bridesmaids a solid and bring a snack tray to share.

Good Ideas:

- ♥ Meat and Cheese Platter
- ♥ Assortment of Nuts
- ♥ Veggies and Dip
- ♥ Crackers and Hummus

Bad Ideas

- ♥ Chips and Salsa (Dripping)
- ♥ Anything with a powder coating (Cheetos, Doritos, etc., they stain clothing).
- ♥ Anything that crumbles easily.

Dresses

Wait to put on your dress as long as possible. Wear a strapless top for your hair and makeup session so you can change without pulling your clothes over your head and smudging the desired effect. Once you put the dress on, there should be no eating, no leaning against walls or trudging through foliage. The dress is not like your jeans; they pick up snags and stains faster than a toddler at the park.

Once you have all donned your dresses, you are warned. Someone will look better in the dress than you. It sucks, but it's true. To make it more awkward, most bridesmaids start complimenting each other on how GOOD the dress looks on YOU. And then you have to return the compliment, which sucks, because you have eyes and you know it looks better on them. It's a vicious cycle that I have no solution to. Sorry.

When you are entrusted with the rings

Normally the maid of honor is holding the groom's ring. If you just hold it, you are likely going to drop it as you arrange the bride's train, hand off bouquets, and perform any of the other duties required. Stick his ring on your finger for security. Most men have big fingers and usually the ring will fit on your thumb.

Sometimes, the bride doesn't quite trust the groomsmen to get her ring down the aisle and will hand her ring off to the maid of honor as well. This happened at a wedding I attended and the groomsmen were freaking out because they thought they had forgotten the ring. They literally were asking the groom's immediate family if they had an extra ring they could borrow.

If you are the maid of honor and have both rings in your possession, give the boys a head's up at the rehearsal dinner.

Pictures

Believe it or not, pictures start as you are getting ready. Everyone is decent, but the photographer joins the bridal party as the final touches are being put on. Typically the photographer will want to get a picture of the mother or father of the bride adjusting the veil. If you are sister or maid of honor to the bride, there is usually a picture of you putting on the bride's shoes for her (awkward and a bit humiliating? Yep). The bride and photographer have usually discussed what they want prior to the day, so just roll with it.

Once everyone is ready there are usually portraits of the bride with each of the attendants separately as well as group photos. You may have to walk to get to a different location for the pictures. In addition to watching your own dress, you may need to hold the bride's train or similarly help her avoid snags and stains.

This is round one of pictures; there will be more posed shots after the ceremony is complete but before the reception begins. As a bridesmaid you will be on the look out for necklaces needing straightening, hair that refuses to stay in its place, 'weird smiles' and whatever else the bride is paranoid about.

Heading Down the Aisle

Hopefully the rehearsal handled any questions on how to get down the aisle. Just a few tips:

- ♥ Don't swing the bouquet. Hold it about waist level.
- ♥ Walk slowly. Usually it is left foot forward, right foot meets left foot, right foot forward. Check with the other bridesmaids if you forget.
- ♥ Stop and smile for the photographer
- ♥ If you are walking with an escort, link arms.
- ♥ When you reach end of the aisle, line up to the left of the altar.

During the Ceremony

Once the ceremony begins, the bridesmaids are supposed to stand and watch the ceremony. You are window dressing to this moment and are not supposed to draw attention to yourself. Accomplish this by not fidgeting. Try to smile and look serene. Don't lock your knees, especially if it is a warm day, you are much more likely to faint and crash into the unity candle. If the bride or maid of honor needs help with something, be ready.

If you are the maid of honor, you have more of a job than just standing there. When the bride reaches the altar, it is your job to adjust her train so that it lays flat and doesn't get tangled up around the bride. Anytime the bride kneels, stands, turns, etc., you are there to adjust that train.

Additionally, after the bride walks down the aisle she is going to hand you her bouquet. If you are adjusting her train, you will need both hands free, so hand off both bouquets to the next bridesmaid in line. She'll hand any she can't handle to the next bridesmaid in line. When you have completed your duty for the bride, you can take both bouquets back.

Should you have a reading, prayer or some other duty in the ceremony, plan to hand your bouquet off to a fellow bridesmaid. At no point should shoving a bouquet under your arm be an option.

Walking Back Up the Aisle

They've kissed and are now wed! Hallelujah! Don't knock the bride down in your haste to get up that aisle! The bride and groom go first and from there it is a reverse order from how you came in. There's no special walking on this one, you can go at a casual pace.

Don't run off to visit with the guests yet! You still have to take pictures with the whole bridal party. You are back on duty for errant necklaces and weird smiles. Expect to be on the job for 45-minutes to an hour.

When in Doubt

- ♥ Bring cash to pay for the hair dresser and makeup artist.
- ♥ Arrange for food and snacks with the other bridesmaids.
- ♥ Remember that the bride gets her way today (in anything).

Odd Facts

Queen Victoria popularized the white wedding dress in her 1840 marriage to Albert of Saxe-Coburg. Until then, brides wore whatever color they felt like.

Chapter 10
The Reception

Entrance

As you've been smiling at the photographer for the last hour, where did all the guests go? Well, they've probably been enjoying some open bar time and are filtering into the reception hall to find their assigned seats. But you don't just walk into the reception hall. Oh, no. You get announced first.

No kidding, you get acknowledged like you are getting a curtain call onstage after a school play. And people clap! The DJ usually does the honors and in a booming voice says something like "And playing the role of the flower girl is... !" When you and the groomsman you were paired with are called, you enter, you wave and you find your respective seats, though you don't sit. Everyone stands when the bride and groom enter the room and are introduced as "Mr. and Mrs. Happily Ever After." Then you can sit.

Sometimes the bride opts for the more traditional receiving line. Basically the wedding party lines up and personally welcomes each of the guests as they filter into the reception. Expect handshakes, hugs, small talk, and achy feet. This ordeal can take awhile.

Once you have made your entrance (or finished your receiving line duties) you will need to find your seat. If there is a head table where the entire wedding party is expected to sit, then it is pretty obvious which direction you are supposed to head. If the wedding party is seeded at tables throughout the party, you are going to need to check with the bride what vicinity of the room you are supposed to be seated. If there are two hundred standing guests when you walk in, it might be a little difficulty picking your seat out of the cheering throngs without a hint which direction you should be looking.

Toasting

Giving a toast was traditionally the purview of the best man. Maid of honor toasting became popularized by Julie Robert's character in "My Best Friend's Wedding" and we've never looked back. I have given amazing toasts and ridiculously awful toasts. Planning is the difference between the two. Try to bring up fond memories of the past and tie them to best wishes for the future. Don't bring up anything that could possibly be embarrassing. Make notes beforehand so you have an idea of what you are going to say and how you are going to say it.

If you screw up, it's okay. Not everyone is a born public speaker. The bride rarely remembers exactly what you said, only how you made her feel at the moment. So no matter what you say, make sure that you speak from your heart and are genuine.

Oh! And don't pull the trigger on that glass of bubbly too quick! Usually the photographer wants a picture of you clinking glasses with the couple before you chug!

Food

In all the toasting and dancing to follow, don't forget to eat! The perk of being a bridesmaid is that the wedding party eats first. If you are seated at a head table, it's served first. If you are seated with the rest of the guests, you are served first at your table. It's been a long time since breakfast. It will be a long time until bed. Do yourself a favor and take the time to eat!

That said, don't eat like a Neanderthal. Put your napkin in your lap. Use the silverware in the order it was meant to be used in. For example, if it is a fancy dinner there will be several forks on the

Don't Ride the Groomsmen!

The wedding is over, the pictures are done, it's time to get the party going. But maybe you have already had a drink or two? Maybe the groomsman has too? Suddenly you have an epic idea.

Let me stop you here. No, you are not going to ride into the reception on the groomsman's back. Nor is he going to ride on yours. It's a bad idea.

Need convincing? Check YouTube for wedding entrance fails. You'll find plenty of reasons why you should keep both feet on the floor!

table. Start with the fork on the left-most side of the plate and work your way in (one fork for each course of food). Small fork at the top of the plate is for dessert. If this entire paragraph makes no sense to you, YouTube "table manners etiquette."

Bustling

The bride has a dress that probably has a train and a lot of extra material layered to fall just right as she walks down the aisle. It looks fantastic in the pictures and by the time the last picture has been snapped, you are already sick of picking it up and fluffing it at every turn. Luckily for you and her, she isn't expected to dance like that. Bustling is a series of buttons and/or ribbons that are used to tuck the train of the dress into a manageable and attractive layer that attaches to the back of her skirt. The seamstress usually invents how this will work for your particular bride. Bustles are confusing and this is something the bride can't really do on her own since she's wearing the dress and the bustle is done at the back of the dress. It is in everyone's best interest if two or three people learn how to bustle the dress from the seamstress, just in case the designated person is unavailable.

Dancing

We all know how to dance, but there are certain traditional dances that come out at weddings. The funky chicken, for one, is always a wedding favorite. Ditto YMCA. I'm not too worried for you on that one. Sometimes the bride takes it into her head to have the whole bridal party do a formal dance together (à la foxtrot or like). That usually involves dance lessons, and is becoming less popular as time goes by. If this is in the cards, your bride will be letting you know way in advance.

You may be going to a wedding that has customs dictated by the culture of either the bride or groom. For example, a Jewish wedding isn't complete without picking the bride and groom up in chairs and dancing them around the room. Some cultures like to link arms and dance in a circle. This one is tons of fun, BUT there is a lot of kicking involved. Either have your shoes strapped on tight or take them off!

I bring all of this up because if there is a cultural heritage involved, it may not ever occur to your bride that you may not be familiar with the tradition, and unlike the wedding, there is no rehearsal for the reception. Basically, when in doubt, ask. The bridesmaids are expected to be out leading the festivities on the dance floor. If there's a possibility there may be a dance you don't know, ask ahead of the big day and then look it up on YouTube! YouTube to the rescue!

Toileting

Of all things, yes we do have to talk about going to the bathroom. Because the bride might need your help! The bustling we talked about above? Yep, the dress is voluminous and NO ONE wants it … uh… involved… in the toilet area. NO YELLOW DRESSES! So it's your job to hold up her skirts on the day. She'll tell you when she needs your help. We all thank you.

Clean Up

When the reception is over and the music stops, don't dash for the door. Stay and see what needs to be done and lend your hands where you can! Most weddings have precious mementos and personal items that need to be collected at the end of the night. Usually the bride and groom will tell their attendants what needs to be taken at the end of the reception and what can be left for the official clean up crew. Think framed pictures, cameras, left over centerpieces (usually they are guest gifts but some get left behind), candleholders and the cake topper. Most of this is entrusted to the maid of honor, mother of the bride or some other responsible party who will make sure it all is returned to the couple after the honeymoon.

When in Doubt

- ♥ Dance the funky chicken with the wedding party.
- ♥ Enjoy the reception.
- ♥ Make small talk and answer questions on the bride's behalf.
- ♥ Give a thoughtful, well-rehearsed toast.

Odd Facts

While Katherine Heigl wore 27 dresses in her famous bridesmaid movie, in real life she has only been a bridesmaid once, for her sister.

Chapter 11
Congratulations!

You made it! The wedding process has been a marathon of events, errands and taffeta. It's exhausting and you deserve a day off, so plan for it. Sleep until noon, read a book or do whatever it is that makes you happy. Your bridesmaid duties are coming to an end, but before you hang up your tulle dress, here are a few notes and tips to finish things right.

Pictures

Most photographers have a "proof" section on their website. Check out the pictures and relive the happy moments of the wedding. While the bride and groom will likely purchase the most prints, you are usually welcome to purchase your own pictures too. Candid pictures with family, friends and loved ones can make great gifts. My sister and I tinted the picture of her and I on her wedding day (à la Kim Anderson) and gave it to our mother for Christmas. Get a memento for yourself too; after all, you worked hard for it!

The Bride's Gift

You love her, remind yourself of that when she presents you with a thank you gift for being a bridesmaid. Swallow the resentment that tastes like bile in the back of your throat. Pretend that you love it, if you can.

F@#% The Knot!

Seriously, the people who write this website have lost their minds. If you are not yet acquainted with The Knot (www.theknot.com) it is a website dedicated to wedding planning, preparation and driving women everywhere to drink. For brides, it has tons of designs and ideas that aren't really practical, as well as reminder email system to make the bride feel behind and insecure about her planning abilities. For bridesmaids, the website offers little; most "bridesmaids" articles are written for the bride so she can better manage her entourage. The few articles written for the bridesmaid offer suggestions such as: After the wedding, pack the brides belongings for the honeymoon, get the dress preserved while the happy couple is gone and stock up the fridge before they return.

Uh. No.

You have dedicated enough time and money to your happy couple. You have done your best to be a good bridesmaid (and we congratulate you!) but your duties end with the reception. Time to spend some time and money on your own life and happiness. The happy couple can buy their own food when they get back!

The gift for the bridesmaid is not touching. It's not thoughtful. On par with the rest of this experience, it will be about her and her big day. Expect inexpensive (read: cheap) earrings or a necklace that she wants you to wear on the day. A bride that splurges will pay for your hair to be done. To her specifications. On her day.

I have yet to receive a gift that was thoughtful to me, the friend, me, the sister that I used beyond HER day. Whatever she gives you, it's probably not "your style." The gift won't reflect the years you've known each other or her appreciation for how much you've done for her and her wedding. Don't forget, this is a thankless job and even your thank you gift will be to her benefit.

Anniversary

Good news! You don't have to buy a gift for the bride and groom on their anniversary! It is nice to send a card however. You bonded with the bride over the creation of her magical day, and built memories in the process. A card acknowledges that the day had meaning for you too, and the event was special for everyone involved. The card can be sweet, it can be funny, it can be whatever you want it to be, just make sure it arrives some time in the two-week window before or week after the anniversary date.

A Life Time of Memories

Hopefully, this has not been too painful of an experience. When you look back at the wedding and the hoopla leading up to it, I hope that you can laugh at the good things and let go of the bad ones. When you see the other bridesmaids, I hope you can be silly, that there is an inside joke or two, a wink over the dinner table. Being part of a wedding can bind the participants together for life and create a circle of friends you never would have picked for yourself, but are bonded to just the same. Embrace your deepened relationship with the bride, and remind her occasionally that her turn at being a bridesmaid will come eventually.

When in Doubt

- ♥ Send a congratulations note on the anniversary.
- ♥ Have a laugh together about the wedding experience and reminisce about the fun times.
- ♥ Don't bring up the brides cold feet, (or dry humping the stripper) ever.

Odd Fact

Each year there are 11 million bridesmaids!

Appendix

I'm not that organized. I kind of do the absolute minimum right up until the last second, and then I scramble and pull the whole thing together like a champ. With that in mind, here are alternative timelines for the real world that will still get the job done!

Bridal Shower

3+ Months Before

- ✓ Guess-timate how many people will be coming
- ✓ Decide where it's going to be and when.
- ✓ Ask the bride if there is anything she can't live with out. Try to include her response in bridal shower plans.
- ✓ Choose a theme.

2 Months Before

- ✓ Send an email to the important guests and tell them to save the date.
- ✓ Purchase bridal shower invitations.
- ✓ Think about games, menu and decorations. Maybe write your ideas down.

1 Month Before

- ✓ Address envelopes. Include important information like gift registry and theme as well as RSVP details.
- ✓ Mail invitations.
- ✓ 2+ Weeks Before
- ✓ Start pulling together decoration pieces. Or at least check to see if they are still in the back of the closet like you vaguely remember.
- ✓ Walk through a bakery and see what kind of cakes they have.
- ✓ Keep a list of RSVP's and confer with the bride if she has been receiving them directly.
- ✓ Decide if you are going to get the bride a gift and what that might be.

1 Weekend Before

- ✓ Shop for decorations, paper goods, and other party props that were actually *not* at the back of the closet.
- ✓ Purchase favors and prizes. Wrap them.
- ✓ Confirm reservations (if applicable).
- ✓ 1 Day Before
- ✓ Buy groceries.
- ✓ Ask the baker to please throw some pink flowers and "Congrats ::bride name here::!" on a sheet cake from the freezer. Take it home with pride.
- ✓ Prepare shower games and activities.
- ✓ Raid Mom's serving platters and tablecloths.
- ✓ Prep food for easy assembly.
- ✓ Bake any desserts that need time to chill overnight or will keep until the next day.
- ✓ Burn a playlist for background music.

✓ Call other bridesmaids in a panic when you realize you've forgotten… whatever you forgot. You know you did. You're completely unorganized.

✓ Run last-minute errands.

Day of:

✓ Prepare menu.

✓ Set up room, arrange chairs etc., for guests.

✓ Pick up balloons.

✓ Raid the neighbors garden for flowers.

✓ Decorate.

✓ Find something somewhat clean and wrinkle-free to wear.

✓ Break into the booze early and take a swig. You totally deserve it.

Bachelorette Party

3+ Months Before

- ✓ Ask the bride what she will absolutely NOT participate in. Everything else is fair game.
- ✓ Guess how many people will be there.
- ✓ Set a date and place.

2 Months Before

- ✓ If you are going for pole dancing lessons, to a male revue, or some other place that will take reservations, make them.
- ✓ Call the bride (again) for the list of invitees.
- ✓ Send out a casual "save the date" email

1 Month Before

- ✓ Email invitations. Texting is okay too. Give guests a head's up if there is a cost involved (the Aussie Thunder From Down Under tickets aren't free, you know).

1 Weekend Before

- ✓ Go to an adult store.
- ✓ Blush uncontrollably.
- ✓ Buy bachelorette party accessories, games, favors and gifts.
- ✓ Figure out a game to play using all the random crap you bought at the adult store.
- ✓ Confirm any "entertainment" you might have scheduled. Oops! Haven't scheduled anything yet? Google to the rescue!
- ✓ Scope out any bars you think you might be going to. Check if there are any specials for bachelorette parties.

1 Day Before

- ✓ Give the bride the head's up on the plan. Keep the details to yourself.
- ✓ Text all of the guests where you are meeting. If you are pub-crawling or traveling in general, text them the second address too. Those bitches are always late.
- ✓ Hydrate.
- ✓ Get plenty of sleep.
- ✓ Day of:
- ✓ Wrap the favors and your gift. (I can't believe you forgot that!)
- ✓ Fill your flask and shove it in the bottom of your purse.
- ✓ Put on your party clothes and makeup.
- ✓ Get to the venue early and decorate with penises (if applicable).
- ✓ Make the bride wear the fake veil all night. It magically waives cover fees and (sometimes) gets free drinks.
- ✓ Enjoy.

Wedding
Once you've agreed to be a bridesmaid...

- ✓ Send a congratulations/engagement card to bride and groom (it will mostly likely end up in her scrapbook).
- ✓ Buy engagement gift and, if applicable, attend the engagement party.
- ✓ Offer to help the bride look at dresses, venues for the ceremony and the reception.

8-10 Months Before

- ✓ Set up an informal get-together of bridesmaids, with the bride of course!
- ✓ Attend wedding shows and expos with the bride.
- ✓ Accompany bride for wedding dress and bridesmaid dress shopping .

6-8 Months Before

- ✓ If the bridesmaid dress is not available for you to try on, get professional measurements taken by a seamstress.
- ✓ Order bridesmaid dress. If it comes from a "David's Bridal" type store, you can walk in and order. Otherwise a bridesmaid might be in charge of collecting and placing orders.
- ✓ Ask the bride about any accessories you need to purchase (shoes, jewelry, wraps).
- ✓ Begin planning bridal shower.

4-6 Months Before

- ✓ Ask the bride about making hotel accommodations.
- ✓ Offer to help the bride stuff, address and puts stamps on invitations. Scope out what other projects are on the horizon and plan accordingly.

2-4 Months Before

- ✓ Throw bridal shower.
- ✓ Begin planning bachelorette party.

✓ Make appointment for bridesmaid's dress fitting (bring shoes and undergarments to be worn at the wedding)

1-2 Months Before

✓ Make appointment for final bridesmaid's dress fitting (bring shoes and undergarments for the wedding).

✓ Offer to help the bride with wedding favors.

✓ Attend the bride's final fitting to learn the bustling for the dress.

✓ Buy wedding present for bride and groom and have it shipped to them.

3 Weeks Before

✓ Throw the bachelorette party.

✓ Start planning a toast for rehearsal dinner and/or reception.

✓ Offer to help bride with any last minute projects.

2 Weeks Before

✓ Prepare the Day-of Emergency Kit

✓ Pick up bridesmaids dress after final alterations

✓ Take a walk in your party shoes to scuff up the bottom. If they hurt right away, this is your chance to either get new shoes or blister patches.

✓ Do any haircut, styling or coloring of your hair.

1 Week Before

✓ Gather items to pack for the wedding.

✓ Practice toast(s) for the rehearsal dinner and/or reception.

✓ Coordinate with bride and let the other bridesmaids know when/ where to meet for rehearsal.

✓ Organize snacks for the primping room.

✓ If applicable, eyebrow waxing and/or spray tan.

2 Days Before

- ✓ Wrestle the to-do list away from the bride. Divvy it up between bridesmaids and knock it out.
- ✓ Pull cash from the ATM. Keep in mind no host bars, professional make-up and hair stylists as well as the "money dance" and any random taxis you might need to escape into.

1 Day Before:

- ✓ Show up early for the rehearsal.
- ✓ Attend the rehearsal dinner.
- ✓ Keep the bride company the night before her big day. Bring Valium, if necessary.

Available September 1, 2015:

"A wicked twist on a classic."

"Flawless."

Quirky!

Available in Print and eBook at all major retailers

About the Author

Jaqueline Kyle is never a bride and always the maid of honor. She enjoys drinking with her fellow bridesmaids and making fun of whoever the current bride happens to be. She lives in California with her two cats and is likely to die unmarried, buried in one of her god-awful maid of honor dresses. She'd love to hear your feedback and stories from your bridesmaid's duties. Email her at ftheknot@hotmail.com